Colin Firth

Colin Firth

The Biography

ALISON MALONEY

Michael O'Mara Books Limited

First published in Great Britain in 2011 by
Michael O'Mara Books Limited
9 Lion Yard
Tremadoc Road
London SW4 7NQ

A CIP catalogue record for this book is available from the British Library.

Papers used by Michael O'Mara Books Limited are natural, recyclable products made from wood grown in sustainable forests. The manufacturing processes conform to the environmental regulations of the country of origin.

ISBN: 978-1-84317-688-6 in hardback print format
ISBN: 978-1-84317-717-3 in trade paperback format
ISBN: 978-1-84317-720-3 in EPub format
ISBN: 978-1-84317-721-0 in Mobipocket format

1 2 3 4 5 6 7 8 9 10

www.mombooks.com

Cover design by Ana Bjezancevic
Designed and typeset by Ana Bjezancevic

Printed in the UK by CPI Mackays, Chatham, ME5 8TD

CONTENTS

FOREWORD

THE MOMENT I fell for actor Colin Firth was not, as it was with most fervent fans, the iconic scene when he emerged dripping and indignant from the pond in *Pride and Prejudice*. It was when he proved his heroic worth by coming to my rescue, in real life, and being every inch the gentleman off the screen as he was on.

The occasion was a press junket for *St. Trinian's* at a posh London hotel, where Colin was paired up with the executive producer and co-star Rupert Everett for all interviews. Despite the boarding school remake being his own project, Rupert appeared, looking unshaven and grumpy, in a shell suit, and slumped in his seat with little more than a glare in my direction. By contrast, Colin, casually dressed in a black jumper and smart jeans, greeted me with a winning smile and a warm welcome.

Throughout the interview, every time Rupert responded to my questions with a monosyllabic and sullen tone, his charming co-star jumped in with chatty, frank and downright witty replies.

As the interview drew to a close I felt an overwhelming rush of gratitude for this self-effacing star, who laughs off his 'sex-god' image and greets plaudits and awards with a look of slight embarrassment. And I was smitten.

We have met many times, before and since, and he is never less than enthralling. A devoted family man with a deep-seated perspective and a strong sense of injustice when it comes to political matters, Colin is intelligent, articulate and friendly. While writing this biography, and in talking to many actors and directors who have worked with Colin throughout the years, a picture emerges of a hugely likeable man who commands both respect and affection from everyone he meets.

Despite fame, fortune and female adulation he remains a truly charming man.

INTRODUCTION

'DARCY? BUT ISN'T he supposed to be sexy?' This damning indictment was Jonathan Firth's reaction to brother Colin's casting in *Pride and Prejudice.*

Yet in 1995 his taciturn romantic hero made TV history when he emerged from an impromptu dip in the lake, with the merest glimpse of flesh showing through his soaking-wet white shirt. Half the nation swooned and the thirty-five-year-old actor became the thinking woman's sex symbol, taking on a persona that was to prove both a blessing and a curse in the years to come.

Now the Oscar-winning star of *The King's Speech*, Colin's life has been one of contradictions. He is the quintessential Englishman who spent his early life in Nigeria and a year in the States, has an Italian wife and a Canadian son. He is perceived as a public school toff, even though he went to a secondary modern in Hampshire. He is the romantic lead who has had only three serious girlfriends and is devoted to his wife; the rom-com star who prefers dark, twisted characters to comedy.

A nomadic childhood in Nigeria, Missouri, Essex and Winchester left Colin feeling like an outsider and yet, by forcing him to change in order to blend in, steered him towards his chosen career. Before he had finished drama school, Colin had been cast in a hit West End play, which resulted in a film role, and he hasn't stopped working since. Picking up his Oscar for *The King's Speech* in 2011, he joked, 'I have a feeling my career just peaked.' In fact it was the highest pinnacle of the many he conquered throughout his career, which had often seen him reach the verge of greatness, only for him to come across another trough.

'I have this weird thing where I keep getting discovered,' he says. '*Another Country* was a break for me, then *Tumbledown* was another break. Everyone talked about the fact that nobody knew me until then, then Darcy came along and the same was said again. Then *Bridget Jones* – and still no one knew me.'

When offered the part of the dashing Mr Darcy in *Pride and Prejudice*, Colin was thirty-four, and considered himself past the age of the romantic lead. But his smouldering performance – and that iconic lake scene – set him on a path that would take him from heart-throb to national treasure, through roles as Renée Zellweger's suitor in *Bridget Jones's Diary*, one of three potential fathers in *Mamma Mia!* and grieving university professor in *A Single Man*.

But it was his portrayal of stammering monarch George VI in *The King's Speech* that would bring Colin out of the shadow cast by Jane Austen's hero. At fifty, Colin is happier than he's ever been. He has a beautiful wife and three sons, whom he adores, his career is soaring and his mantelpiece is groaning with awards. And the aristocratic Mr Darcy has finally been trumped by a king.

This book traces the highs and lows of the esteemed actor's life and career, from his unconventional childhood and unhappy schooldays, the college days that turned him around and his early career. We trace the inside story of his rift with Rupert Everett, his playful rivalry with Hugh Grant, his years in the wilderness with Meg Tilly and the moment he fell in love with his stunning Italian wife, Livia. Find out about the causes that move him to direct action and the family that keep him grounded.

The first ever biography traces the route from Hampshire to Hollywood, via stately homes and sumptuous palaces, and gives a true insight into one of Britain's greatest actors.

CHAPTER I

Out of Africa

O N A WARM, sunny day in 1995, Colin Firth stood by a cool, clear lake in the grounds of Cheshire's beautiful Lyme Hall. As the cameras started to roll he slowly stripped off his jacket and waistcoat for the scene that would change his life for ever.

Yet, ringing in his ears were the words of his younger brother and one or two female friends who had expressed amazement at his casting as the 'dashing and handsome' Mr Darcy in the BBC's production of *Pride and Prejudice*. Secretly, the thirty-four-year-old agreed with their harsh assessment.

'I am totally unlike him,' he told the *Daily Express* some years later. 'He was this taciturn, dark, sexy guy and that is just not me. He rode horses and owned a wonderful home in Derbyshire. I ride a bike, talk a lot and do not live in luxury.

'I nearly turned it down because I could not have been more wrong for the role. And that one decision, had I gone ahead with it, would have changed my life.'

Mr Darcy's impromptu dip, and subsequent stilted conversation with Elizabeth Bennet as he stood, dripping and abashed, in a white shirt and breeches, would become one of the most iconic scenes in TV history. But it was to prove a double-edged sword. While launching a career which most fledgling actors can only dream of, Darcy was to become a 'part-time burden' which would stay with him for the next fifteen years. Journalists would raise the name of Austen's surly hero in every interview, casting directors would struggle to see beyond the curly mop and white breeches, and even his wife Livia would tease him when he clambered out of bed looking less than perfect with a cheeky, 'Oh look, it's Mr Darcy!'

'It got my name recognized but it also put me in a box,' he told *The Times* in 2007. 'Things were going well; I was building a diverse working life. Twelve years on it feels like a school nickname you can't shake. It occurred to me the other day to change my name to Mr Darcy and be done with it.'

The part had him pigeonholed as 'posh totty', the strong, silent type. He was the quintessentially English heart-throb with the cut-glass accent and, many assumed, a wealthy family and public school upbringing. In fact, the public perception of Colin Firth was way off the mark. The future star had a nomadic childhood in Africa, England and America and a chequered education in a variety of state schools. A search back into the Firth line shows no links to landed gentry and no Jane Austen-style fortune. As Colin himself asserts, 'I don't own a horse or acres of property. I'm a secondary-modern school kid with no links to nobility. Yet I played this taciturn, dark, sexy guy and everyone remembers it.'

• • •

Colin's parents, David Norman Lewis Firth and Shirley Jean Rolles, were both born in India where their own parents were missionaries. His paternal grandfather, Cyril Bruce, was an ordained minister and the son of a wool merchant from Huddersfield. Shortly after graduating from Cambridge in 1930, he moved to the Indian province of Bellary, where he would preach for nineteen years.

Shirley's father, who went by the rather grand name of Montague John Rolles, was the son of a Bournemouth butcher named Montague Rolles Rolles and descended from farming stock. Montague Jr and wife Helen were Congregationalist ministers when they arrived in India, during the rule of the British Raj, and they soon became involved in the Church of South India, of which Cyril was a founding member. Shirley and David met through the organization when they were three and five respectively. However, after a disagreement with the Church, Montague decided to divert his energy from religion to medicine and become an osteopath. To qualify, he moved his family to Iowa in the United States, where he would study for seven years before returning to India to set up a practice there.

Although Colin's four grandparents were missionaries, and his paternal grandfather an ordained minister, he insists that 'they weren't the sort of missionaries who went around converting the natives and bashing people over the head with Christianity'.

For their part, Colin's parents chose academic careers, with David joining the RAF as a student teacher, with the rank of flight officer, before becoming a history lecturer and Shirley, perhaps as a result of her devout background, choosing the specialist field of alternative comparative religions. They wed in 1958 at the Congregational Church in Battersea, where

Shirley was living while studying for her degree. She went on to become a university lecturer but continued to study, publishing a PhD on death and bereavement in the Gujarati community in Southampton, for which she learned Hindi, in 1997.

Colin was the eldest of three, born in 1960 in Grayshott, Hampshire. Within two weeks his transient lifestyle began with a long journey to Africa. David had taken a teaching post in Nigeria and the family were to move there for four years. Colin's younger sister Kate was born in the West African country two years later.

Being a very young boy when the family returned to England, Colin has sketchy memories of his time in Nigeria, but he can recall feeling miffed as he watched his dad travelling to the local high school to work. 'I remember very clearly my father driving to work in a Beetle,' he told *The Guardian* in 2001. 'There was a dirt road that went perpendicular to the house and I would watch him go. I could still see him when he parked the car outside the school – it wasn't far, but an unpleasant walk in the African sun. He was a little dot. And I remember thinking: "What's he got to do there that's better than hanging around with me?"'

He was not without his friends, however, and spent much of his time playing with an African boy called Godfrey. To his embarrassment, Colin later recalled 'him trying to persuade me to come round to his place, and me being scared to go'.

While memories of those African years are few, the time spent there laid an important foundation stone in the building of Colin's character. It taught him awareness of other cultures and sympathy for less affluent lifestyles which spilled over into his adult life when he became a passionate advocate of human rights and champion of asylum seekers.

'It did make an impression on me, not least because people we'd known there continued to be in our lives as visitors,' he said. 'And there were constantly people from India so there was an immense cultural diversity under my own roof throughout my entire upbringing, and I consider that to be absolutely nothing but a privilege.'

On their return to England, the family moved to Chelmsford in Essex, and four-year-old Colin was sent to the local primary school. After the freedom he had learned to love in Africa, the rules and regulations of an English state school seemed stifling and somewhat baffling to the new pupil. 'I didn't take kindly to being sent to school, to this rather cold place where you're given lots of instructions and nobody loves you,' he said on *Desert Island Discs*. 'You're sort of on your own. I couldn't believe I had to go back again the next day, I remember that. I thought, "My first day of a school is over, thank God for that. Now I can get on with my childhood." And day two was a horrible shock.'

Colin's dislike of school would dog him throughout his education, but it didn't take him long to discover the one activity into which he could put his heart and soul. The revelation came when he was cast as Jack Frost in the school pantomime, at the age of five. The acting bug had bitten and the future Mr Darcy was getting a taste of great things to come. 'I was in a pair of silver satin pants, a blue satin sash and, portentously, a billowing white shirt,' he recalls. 'I was a hit. I don't know that I've been as much of a hit since, and I thought, "That is where the love and attention lies." There was nothing else that gave me that level of praise and approval.'

As a mediocre student, the lure of the lights, the potential to impress and the need to relieve the boredom of everyday lessons appealed to the young Colin. He eagerly auditioned for any production open to him and would take any role, no matter how small. 'I had tiny parts in all the stuff I did, but I loved it,' he says. 'That's what made me apply to drama school and want to become an actor.'

The new-found love of acting also helped him settle into school and get along better with his peers. Having spent his first four years in Africa, learning his precise English accent from his parents and their friends, he was a stranger to the more common elements of Essex dialect and found it shocking. His first real job as an aspiring actor was to emulate his classmates.

'Accents were an issue,' he told *The Times* in 2007. 'It was a shock to hear aitches being dropped. I felt like a freak speaking with the accent I had. So I changed it and only started to speak like this when I was in the sixth form.'

The birth of second sibling Jonathan, in April 1967, completed the family. Although the brothers are the best of pals today, an age gap of over six years meant that Colin was closer to sister Kate as they grew up. 'Colin left home when I was eleven, so it was a big gap,' says Jonathan. 'It's only as we've got older that we've become closer.'

As the oldest sibling, he was a protective big brother who looked after the little ones and loved to amuse them. 'We were competitive but also protective of one another,' remembers Kate. 'At infant school he gave me instructions not to leave until he collected me from the classroom. At break he always made sure I had enough money to buy a Thunderbirds chocolate bar.'

Although they both held good academic posts, David and Shirley were thrifty and instilled in Colin a sense of frugality that would see him shun the trappings of obvious or ostentatious wealth in later years. He is still, he reveals, 'conditioned to save silver foil because it used to be expensive'. But he admits their prudence was often irritating to him as a child. 'It annoyed me sometimes that they weren't more avaricious. I would like to have had more gadgets in the house, more expensive toys.'

They encouraged their children to think and read and they were rarely allowed to watch television at home. Instead, Colin spent his Saturday mornings learning to play the piano and would entertain Jonathan and Kate with jokes, shows and impressions. 'He loved acting out from the time he was at school,' says mum Shirley. 'The big thing then was Batman, so Colin was Batman all the time and I had to make him a costume.'

Kate would join in the dressing-up games and make up little stories with her brother. 'I was the princess in jumble-sale ballgowns, he was the prince in cloak and breeches.'

A rare treat would be permission to watch *Top of the Pops*, and one particular performance by Marc Bolan, singing 'Hot Love', left a lasting impression on the wide-eyed ten-year-old. 'I loved all the glitter and corkscrew hair,' he said. 'I wanted to be rock and roll and not to grow up and wear a suit.'

After moving around Essex for four years the Firths returned to Hampshire, the county of Colin's birth, when he was eight. His father took a job as a lecturer at King Alfred's College in Winchester and the family settled in Alresford, a picturesque Georgian town on the banks of the River Arle, just outside the city, which was voted *Country Life*'s favourite market town in 2007. Shy Colin had another first day at school to get through, at the local Dean Primary School, and this time he would be going into an established class. Yet again, Colin would turn chameleon to fit in.

'It had been astonishing to me in my first ever school in Essex that the kids didn't talk as my parents did, in BBC "received pronunciation",' he said later. 'Just when I thought I'd mastered the Essex accent, I was in a Hampshire school. And later America. So, strangely enough, I became an actor.'

Still a reluctant student, he did find inspiration at school in the form of teacher Chris Pines, who went on to become the mayor of Winchester. Taking on the 'generally disgruntled pupil' at the age of ten, the young form tutor, only in his twenties himself, managed to engage Colin in a way none of his predecessors had.

'He's the most wonderful teacher I ever had,' Colin told the *Hampshire Chronicle*. 'He loved the kids. He loved teaching. He inspired my interest in education. He made teaching and learning exciting and I remained friends with him for many years afterwards.'

While other teachers in the school used threats and punishments, including the cane, Chris used encouragement and humour. 'He was incredibly approachable,' said Colin in the *Times Educational Supplement*. 'He maintained discipline through wit rather than any sort of rod or threat of detention. I was quite porous to new ideas at that age. He taught, and I soaked up, everything to do with grammar, writing, dinosaurs and the prehistoric age.

'We had corporal punishment at the school: usually a whack on the hand with a ruler or cane. I remember in one art class Chris was cutting paper at the front and he called me up because I talked too much. He told me to hold out my hand and I thought, "This isn't like him." I was really quite scared for a moment. I held out my hand and he told me to hold out the other one as well. He then put a bin bag in my hands and poured his rubbish in.'

Chris, who was reunited with his former pupil in 2007 when Colin was presented with an honorary degree from the University of Winchester, remembers an animated and sociable lad.

'He was an exuberant, lively, interested child,' he says. 'He wanted to know everything that was going on around him and he was keen, but not necessarily academically minded. He enjoyed his social life.'

One thing Colin didn't enjoy was the school dinners. The stodgy meals of the sixties put him off meat and he objected to the dinner ladies making him sit at the table until he had eaten every last morsel. 'We were always being reminded of "the starving people in Africa",' he told *The Observer*. 'I remember thinking at the time that even they wouldn't eat this. I'd leave the dining hall with a pocketful of sausages and tinned peas. I preferred it being there than in my stomach.'

In spite of Mr Pine's best efforts, and his academic background, Colin failed his eleven-plus, meaning a grammar school place was out of the question. And before he could settle into a secondary school the Firths were on the move again. In 1972, when Colin was eleven, David accepted an exchange year, teaching at a college in St. Louis, Missouri. The family packed up their things and flew to America, along with a large group of fellow teachers embarking on a similar adventure. For Colin, the year in Missouri was to prove the best and worst of times. At the local high school he was moved up a year because the education system in the UK began a year earlier than the US. However, the leap meant he was the least mature in the year group and he felt awkward around the older boys. In a class of boys with long hair and earrings who would bring drugs to school on a regular basis, Colin was an outsider, seen as an English geek. 'I was still into train sets,' says Colin. He struggled once more to fit in but he is the first to admit that his tendency to get lippy didn't help matters.

'American kids were a hell of a lot more sophisticated,' he told *The Observer*. 'I was barely out of grey shorts. I'd come out of primary school, where my classmates had grass-stained knees and collected football cards. They were more like something out of *Woodstock*. I was like something out of *Just William*. They had slogans on their backs that were to do with the Vietnam War. I felt like a geek. I made up for it with a false cockiness. Before I got rejected, I would tell someone to fuck off. Someone would say, "What's your name?" and I'd say, "Mind your own business."'

The 'subtle isolating behaviour' of two or three members of his class had a surprising effect on his grades. Despite his unhappiness, the struggling student was suddenly A-grade material thanks to some fantastic teachers and a lot of time spent on his own. Colin's former teacher Carol Welstahoff remembered him as a studious child who always had his head in a book.

'The others kids didn't take to him because he was different. To them, he was your stereotypical English schoolboy. I think it was a lonely time, but he spent a lot of it reading. He was a very conscientious, top-of-the-class student.'

Away from school, however, things were more interesting for the curious lad. In the extended school holidays, David and Shirley took the children on long trips around the United States in an old Volkswagen camper van. On their first trip, over the Christmas break, they travelled south, through Mississippi and Tennessee, stopping at Memphis, and then on to Baton Rouge in Louisiana. Another journey saw them heading east to Arizona, through Kansas and New Mexico. Colin adored the trips and marvelled at the many different landscapes the old bus trundled through.

'There are so many versions of the planet on one continent,' he says. 'Everything from the landscape to the vegetation to the people blew me away. Americans are bursting with warmth and friendliness. When our old Volkswagen broke down – which it did frequently – people fixed our car and offered us hospitality with no expectations. It's something Europeans don't realize unless they've travelled the real small-town America.'

Shirley remembered the seven years she had spent growing up in Iowa, so felt at home in the States. Being firm believers that travel broadened the mind, she and David were determined to show their children as much of the country as they could squeeze into a year's visit.

'They were extremely keen to expose us to those sorts of experiences and to open up the world to us, and not just be focused on one's own postal district,' remembers Colin.

They were happy family times, sharing the wide-open spaces of the American countryside and sleeping at night in the cramped interior of the VW camper. But Shirley remembers one hairy moment when Colin's adventurous streak left her panic-stricken. 'I have a memory of Colin walking along the edge of a wall, obviously testing us out, because the amount of adrenalin I used up in that moment was colossal. We were all petrified because it was a mile down if he had fallen, but this was somebody who was very daring.'

Colin's time in America was, he says, a 'decisive year' but much of it, especially the school days, remains a 'hideous memory'. Twenty years on, he would return to his old high school in St. Louis where he was somewhat relieved to find it was 'pretty nasty. The place was horrible and had the atmosphere of a reform school. It made me realize that it wasn't all me.'

By the age of thirteen, when the Firth family finally settled in Hampshire for good, Colin was a well-travelled boy. But from the perspective of a teenager, desperate to fit in somewhere, that didn't always feel like an advantage. 'People always feel alone at some point in their lives, definitely,' he told the *Daily Express*.

'Childhood can be pretty grim in that way. We travelled a lot and though I consider the travelling to be the single most enriching feature of my childhood, the down side is that there is an element of loneliness.'

But Colin had picked up more than a slightly cocky attitude during his time in the States, and his return to his homeland was not going to be easy.

CHAPTER 2

Acting Up

AFTER THEIR AMERICAN adventure, Colin's family arrived back in Winchester in 1973, the year of glam rock. David Bowie was the biggest-selling artist since the Beatles, Mick Jagger was voted Best Dressed Man and Slade were rocking the charts. Colin's first rock heroes, T-Rex, were enjoying hits with '20th Century Boy' and 'The Groover' and stars were wearing more make-up than their female fans. On the fashion scene, platforms and flares were everywhere and big hair was bang on trend.

At the difficult age of thirteen, with so many other distractions, the last thing Colin wanted to be doing was joining yet another new school. And his attempts to blend in at St. Louis had left an unwelcomed legacy. His new classmates at Montgomery of Alamein school in Winchester immediately dubbed him 'the Yank' because of his Missouri twang and Colin chastised himself for being 'feeble minded' enough to have picked up an accent in the year away.

The image of Colin as a posh pupil at a top public school, which many in the past have inferred from the cut-glass accent he now uses, is miles from the truth. Montgomery of Alamein may have been a boys' school but it was also a secondary modern state school with some fairly rough inhabitants. The accents were rural Hampshire and the language far from the world of Jane Austen. 'It was "Firthy, come and get a smack in the mouth" and "Who you fucking looking at?" he told *The Times*. 'I wouldn't have survived sounding as I do now.'

The isolation was not helped by Colin's ignorance of popular culture. His parents refused to let him watch commercial television, allowing only BBC programmes into the home. As a result he was excluded from playground conversations on the most popular shows, such as *Crossroads*, *Randall and Hopkirk (Deceased)*, and even *Magpie*. As well as a difficult time with the pupils, the actor maintains that most of the teachers at the school despised him and were convinced he would amount to nothing. His form tutor once informed him he would be lucky if he ended up working in a shoe shop.

On another occasion he scored three per cent in a chemistry test, being awarded two points for writing his name and two points for the teacher's name – then losing one for spelling Sir's name incorrectly!

Added to the mix was the fact that Colin was going through puberty in a boys' school, something that had not escaped him at the time. 'I was not crazy about being at an all boys' school,' he told the *Daily Express* in 2007. 'Girls, to me, looked fantastic but out of reach. So I think that added to the general mood of being an awkward adolescent.'

While intelligent, he found school didn't teach the subjects he was interested in. For example, while they were studying Thomas Hardy and Jane Austen, he was more interested in Existentialist writers such as Albert Camus. When he asked if he could learn guitar at school, he was told that wasn't a 'serious instrument' and offered the baritone euphonium instead.

'My education was deeply stifling,' he says. 'Nothing that I had experienced in the classroom has had anything to do with life. At that age your entire being is invaded by your sexual consciousness, and all you're getting is algebra and French. I'm delightfully happy as an adult, but I was not very happy as a child. I'm very suspicious of people who romanticize their childhood.'

Dad David recalls, 'He would have found it difficult fitting in at any school – partly because of moving and partly because he wanted to go off and follow his own interests.'

School pal Arron Reilly remembers Colin was much happier out of school, experiencing the outdoors: 'We used to go camping together, get a tent and go walking,' he revealed. 'We would talk about girls but we weren't brilliantly successful with them. I think we were both a bit scared of them.'

Colin's reaction to the rigid education he so despised was a quiet rebellion, starting with the occasional day bunking off with Arron. 'We would sneak off to the fields and have a fag,' says his old friend. 'Colin didn't like school. He didn't get into a lot of trouble, although he did bunk off.'

Colin admits he was 'quietly resistant', choosing to opt out and pay little attention rather than openly challenge authority. He was, he says, 'neither an identifiable wild rebel nor someone who toed the line in a meaningful way. I didn't really like the system, I didn't like the education. I didn't fight it very courageously. I just didn't go along with it very much. 'My rebellions were sneaky, passive. I didn't smash windows or get into fights: if I did I was strictly on the receiving end.'

The late headmaster, Dennis Beacham, ran a tight ship at the school and told the pupils, 'Don't whinge, don't moan, don't tell me you're tired. I'm tired too.' Colin's passive protest made little impression on Dennis, who pointed out, a tad spikily. 'He was a somewhat quiet, withdrawn boy, academically moderate,' he said. 'By and large, he passed through school without any colour at all. He made no impact on the school.'

As in primary school, however, Colin remembers one special teacher who did manage to spark his interest in a subject, and had faith in his ability to make something of his life. Angela Kirby, who has since passed away, taught English language and used humour and drama to grab her pupils' attention.

'She was a creature of the theatre,' recalled Colin in the *Times Educational Supplement*. 'She had quite a camp, wicked wit, with a shock of bright white hair and flowing velvet dresses. She didn't suffer fools gladly and would use humour and gentle teasing on us pupils.'

In a class full of sexually maturing boys in a single-sex school, the flamboyant teacher caused quite a stir, despite her advanced age. 'It was strange to fancy her – she must have been at least fifty and she was no beauty – but we all did,' says Colin. 'I think it was her friskiness and sophistication we liked.'

Most importantly, however, she ignited a spark of interest in the disgruntled pupil and, when other teachers wrote him off, she was convinced he was university material. She would nurture the young enthusiastic reader to an A at O level.

Despite his lack of academic prowess in other departments, young Colin harboured ambitions to become a doctor. All that changed when a bout of illness in his early teens fired up Colin's thirst for literature. While no doubt revelling in the opportunity to skip school, he was also devouring all the books in the house, including Homer's notoriously difficult tomes *The Iliad* and *The Odyssey*, a precis of which he had first come across in *Look and Learn* magazine. 'I felt it was something that should be capitalized on and he did one of his O levels in English literature early,' says mum Shirley. 'He was reading everything that we had. He got very interested in Greek mythology.' With the help of another passionate teacher, Stanley Payne, he took the early exam and passed with flying colours.

While his new-found passion for reading was a genuine escape for the budding actor, he also had a less angelic motive and later admitted, 'I took refuge in books with the hope of getting laid by name-checking Dostoevsky.'

Throughout his schooling, Colin maintained his love of acting but even that left him in a dilemma within the confines of the school. While he loved performing in school plays he felt foolish in front of his peers and explains that 'it wasn't exactly the cool thing to do'. He threw his energies, instead, into extracurricular drama and swapped his Saturday morning piano lessons for acting classes. Writer and actress Freda Kelsall, a friend of Shirley's, was in the process of setting up a weekend acting school in the local community centre and encouraged all three Firth children to join.

'We had no idea that for each of them it was to help decide their future careers,' says Freda. 'Colin was fourteen then, energetic, committed and inventive. As the eldest, he needed to decide sooner what he wanted to do with his life, and I began coaching him for drama school external exams. I always believed he'd do well.'

Freda, who still writes and performs in Hebden Bridge, Yorkshire, was to coach the lad throughout his teens and has remained friends with him. The loyal star is quick to credit her contribution to his success and remains grateful for her tutelage. 'He doesn't court celebrity, but tries to use it to the advantage of others,' she comments in the *Hebden Times*. 'He's good company, honest and generous, an acute observer, very funny, yet deeply thoughtful, as he was as a teenager.

'He often credits his Saturday morning classes and early coaching in interviews, and surprises me sometimes. He says I taught him "the reality of the inner world", and when I saw *The King's Speech* I understood what he may have meant by it.'

Best pal Arron Reilly also shared his enthusiasm for amateur dramatics and together they appeared regularly in plays in the village hall at Ropley, near Alresford.

'Colin had bigger roles than me but he didn't give me any idea he wanted to be an actor,' says his childhood friend in *The Sun*. 'He was interested in the arts, and we would mimic things like Monty Python.'

Again, the reason for throwing himself into am-dram was in part motivated by a desire to mingle with the opposite sex.

'I have a feeling that part of the reason for me doing amateur dramatics was to meet girls,' admits Colin. 'The girls were good-looking and it was a way, quite frankly, to get laid. I joined a band, I acted and I read books with fancy names.'

Despite his ulterior motives, Colin was beginning to think of acting as a future career. And one particular actor, the late, great Paul Scofield, was to cement his decision. Colin watched his Oscar-winning performance as Thomas More in *A Man For All Seasons* at the age of fourteen and was blown away.

'It made me reassess what acting was,' he told Sue Lawley on *Desert Island Discs*. 'It was nothing to do with demonstration, it was nothing to do with anything I was conscious of in body language; it was just an expression of integrity and there was a such a paradox in that because acting by its very nature is false. So how can this man, through doing very little, exude truth and humanity and intelligence? I was so fascinated by that and that's basically what I've tried to pursue ever since.'

In a blinding moment of clarity, aged fourteen, Colin Firth knew what he wanted to do with the rest of his life. He made 'an announcement to himself' that he was going to be an actor, no matter how much the odds were stacked against him. 'That was a slightly euphoric moment, really and I felt very liberated from the drudgeries,' he revealed to the *Irish Times*. 'It made me feel very grand.'

Having let the delicious idea sink in, Colin delighted in telling his school friends his new ambition and admits that it allowed him an excuse to shirk his detested schoolwork. But the more he repeated his goal, the more serious he got about it and finally he steeled himself to break the news to his parents. As two academics who placed high value on the importance of education, he was prepared for some resistance and knew they would be disappointed that he wasn't following a more traditional university route.

'They were frightened because that was the only route they knew,' he said, talking on *Desert Island Discs* 'They weren't being snobbish about my desire to be an actor, I really believe that. They were just concerned about the first member of the family ever going on that completely unknown route.'

But Colin's obvious enthusiasm for treading the boards swayed his parents and they were soon backing his ambition.

'I think my feeling was, well, if this is what he wants to do, and he's got some enthusiasm, then thank God he's found something he's interested in,' remembers David.

Shirley agrees. 'We both felt that it really was important that children should follow their dream,' she says. 'This was his dream – and he was very committed right from the start.'

Because of his hatred of formal education, as he knew it, Colin was keen to distance himself from the academic world of his mum and dad. Like every teenager, he was finding his own identity and eager to make his own mark. He grew his hair long, pierced his ears, bought himself some flared jeans and joined the last throes of the hippy movement.

Past guitar lessons, which had proved a disappointment because the teacher chose folk and classic tunes rather than the latest Jimi Hendrix track, still proved useful when Colin decided to form a band with his mates, playing and singing on covers from rock groups such as The Doors. He and pal Arron listened to prog rock groups in Colin's bedroom and were big fans of King Crimson, Yes and Pink Floyd. Used to being an outsider, Colin stuck to his guns when the punk movement began to engulf the youth of Britain in the mid-seventies although he does admit that, having grown his hair and become a latter-day hippy, he felt 'slightly stranded' by the irreverent new trend.

'Progressive rock had become so pompous, and that pompousness suited me, because I had become so well acquainted with it,' he told *The Observer*. 'There was so much snobbery. It was my sanctuary from the laddishness that I didn't fit in with.'

At home, things were often fiery between the difficult youth and his parents, but his behaviour was hardly off the scale of teenage rebellion. He tried drinking and smoking and hung out at music festivals with his pals. He got into one or two fights, usually with friends or classmates, rather than strangers. However the family rows were the usual small frictions between a sullen teenager and a parent. 'It was a whole series of things and was as much as to do with what he suspected. It wasn't one incident.' The majority of the squabbles, he says, 'were about washing dishes and homework. There wasn't a massive meltdown.'

Colin's father put the minor misdemeanours down to the same headstrong nature that often got Colin into scrapes with his peers at school. His self-confessed tendency to mouth off when others would back down was often the cause of his woes. 'He showed that he did have a strong personality and stood out for the wrong reasons,' David says. 'Nevertheless, I do think that kids who show they can hold an audience are sometimes troublesome and should perhaps try for acting.'

Leaving Montgomery school with average O-level results, Colin went on to Barton Peveril Sixth Form College in Eastleigh, six miles outside Winchester, to study for his English literature, religious studies and drama A levels. His two years there, from 1977 to 1979, were to turn his life around. For the first time in his school career, he discovered learning could be fun, thanks once again to an inspirational tutor.

In 2010 English teacher Penny Edwards was to accompany her star pupil to the House of Commons where he was presented with a Gold Award from the Association of Colleges in recognition of his achievements since leaving the college. But for now, Penny was the catalyst that spurred him on to greater things.

'I really value what college did for me,' he said at the ceremony. 'Barton Peveril College saved me. I've always felt very grateful for the extraordinary level of faith they managed to maintain in me.

'It's left me with a belief that everybody deserves a second chance. My two years at Barton Peveril were among the two happiest years of my life. I must have been paying some attention as I can still quote randomly from Thomas Hardy and Lord Byron.'

Colin arrived at the college with long hair, an earring, and a penchant for flares and lairy waistcoats. Penny, whose career at the establishment spanned thirty-six years until her retirement in 2010, remembers Colin as an intelligent, focused and determined lad.

'Colin was very sensitive to literature and had this stage presence,' she said. 'I wasn't surprised he did so well. Underneath the laddish exterior was quite a shrewd character who knew exactly what he wanted to do.'

The tutors soon picked up on his natural talent for drama and those who saw him starring in the college productions of *Sweeney Todd* and Molière's *Scapino* and were bowled over.

'He was a lively and laid-back teenager who had an ability to dominate the stage,' reveals Penny. 'In those days I think he will admit he was not that interested in the academic side but very keen on learning as much as he could about practical acting.'

With his love of rock music and his eclectic reading material, Colin found this was the first time he 'slotted in very nicely with the in-crowd' although he admits to a dodgy fashion sense. 'I used to wear Rupert trousers,' Colin cringed some time later. 'Big flared tartan trousers. Revolting. And, God, my seventies hair's enough to spend my life apologizing for. Vermeer hair. I burned a lot of my photos from the time.'

English Literature classmate John Harrison remembers a

Genesis fan 'with long hair and an army or air force greatcoat and desert boots with an album under his arm – somewhat different to his suave presence now'.

After years of waiting to get close to the opposite sex, the sixteen-year-old Colin was now mixing with girls on a day-to-day basis for the first time and, despite his lack of suaveness, their reaction was a taste of things to come.

Fiona Ackroyd, who studied English literature alongside the future Mr Darcy, was one of the female students who was clearly impressed with her chiselled classmate.

'He was an absolute sweetheart,' she says. 'He was drop-dead gorgeous even then, in the 1979 uniform of army greatcoat and desert boots.'

Faced with this female attention, Colin, perhaps due to spending his teenage years in a boys' school, was a little nonplussed. While friendly and outgoing around the young women, he was a little backward in coming forward when it came to romance.

'He was very sociable and a lot of the girls liked him,' says Penny. 'This really beautiful girl had a terrible crush on him, but they never got together. It became a running joke.'

While the drama and English had improved his attitude to education in general, he still had his moments of rebellion. On one occasion, when he was supposed to be resitting an A level, he decided instead to go back to bed because 'it felt like a treadmill I didn't want to be on'.

Colin was offered university courses conditional on his results, but that decision to stay in bed rather than resit the A level cost him the chance of a place. He admits he has often had fleeting regrets about the missed opportunity.

'For quite a while I felt there was something missing. Somewhere within what I think I would always declare has been my contempt for that, has been a sneaking envy,' he told *The Independent on Sunday*. 'I think I romanticized great seats of learning. I'd read a novel years ago which made me yearn to have gone to either Oxford or Cambridge, preferably in the twenties. You realize the experiences you're getting are more to be cherished than dreams. I do think as one gets older that fantasies, certainly from my point of view, stop outweighing your actual realistic objectives.'

Years later, the question of whether he had disappointed his father by not going to university still weighed on his mind, despite his considerable success.

'My father was worried when I decided not to go to university,' he told *The Independent*. 'But only because he wanted me to be able to find something that was stimulating from which I could make a living. I lit on acting because there really wasn't anything else that seemed feasible.

'I did say to my dad later that I felt like I hadn't fulfilled the family tradition and that I had missed something by not going to university, by not following that path.' His father quickly assuaged his worries. 'He told me that, considering all the things I've learnt for various roles, I haven't missed out on much.'

Looking back, he sees his youthful insurrection as typical teenage idleness but then, he says, it felt like a principled choice.

'I would have gone to university had I not allowed myself to be derailed into moody adolescent laziness,' he maintains to *The Times*. 'I liked to characterize it then as a defiant decision to resist the system. But I was just resistant to schoolwork. If someone wanted me to read Shakespeare, I wanted to read Thomas Mann. If someone tried to make me listen to Brahms, I had to listen to Hendrix.'

While at college, Colin earned some cash as a paperboy and part-time dustman. But when school was done, he felt there was only one place for an aspiring actor to be, and he headed for the bright lights of London.

CHAPTER 3

The Past is Another Country

FOUR YEARS AFTER setting his heart on a career in acting, Colin's college days were over and crunch time had come. He was determined to follow his dream and, in an effort to be close to theatres, Colin left the family home shortly before his nineteenth birthday and travelled to the capital. He had little idea of what a struggling actor's life might entail and he travelled optimistically, 'like Dick Whittington'.

The year was 1979, the dawn of the Thatcherite era and a time of deep unrest for the country's trade unions. One of Colin's favourite bands, Pink Floyd, has just released *The Wall* and Meryl Streep had won the Best Actress Oscar for *Kramer vs Kramer*. Even the most ambitious of eighteen-year-olds wouldn't have dared to predict he would one day co-star with this most fêted of Hollywood actresses.

In a bid to tread the boards, Colin joined the National Youth Theatre where, according to him, he rose to the dizzy heights of 'third fairy on the left'. He found a poorly paid job as stage door keeper at the Shaw Theatre in London's Euston Road where he whiled away the time in his cramped cubbyhole reading Kafka and 'staring into the abyss'.

From there he moved on to the National Theatre, helping out in the wardrobe department and making tea. He would stay behind at night and says he was 'alone in the building, alone in London'. It was a miserable time but Colin managed to stay focused, knowing that being inside theatres gave him the chance to learn about his chosen profession, get to know people involved and, perhaps, open the right doors.

His opportunity came in a conversation with an art director at the theatre, who urged Colin to apply for the Drama Centre, on Prince of Wales Road, Chalk Farm. To his delight, he was accepted. 'It was a salutary moment when I actually went to drama school and realized that this was what I always said I was going to do. No more fall-back,' he told the *Irish Times* in 2003.

The drama school, set up by a breakaway group from the London School of Speech and Drama, specialized in the Stanislavski method of acting, which the creator, Constantin Stanislavski, believed was the key to 'theatrical truth'.

Former principal Christopher Fettes explains: 'The approach, which is Russian, is based on using your inner demons to express the emotions of your character; you turn your own frustration into someone else's.' Colin, he recalls, was a natural receptacle for the system.

The method 'simply doesn't suit the Anglo-Saxon temperament in many, many cases,' Christopher says. 'But he responded to the training on every level, right from the early stages.' The ability to communicate inner struggle without merely using words, previously seen in such greats as Robert De Niro and Dustin Hoffman, would become the basis for his most famous taciturn and 'brooding' characters in the future. It was a logical step on from the 'reality of the inner world' that Freda Kelsall had already instilled in him, but this drama school was no easy ride. The prospectus for the centre, whose other alumni include Pierce Brosnan, Frances de la Tour, Paul Bettany and Tara Fitzgerald, emphasized hard work and dedication.

While he had been an unwilling worker throughout his school career, Colin chose the course because of this very toughness. Now he had his sights set on a successful career, he was prepared to put all his energy into making it happen. At last he understood the power of learning, and of striving to achieve his goal.

'I chose the Drama Centre because it had a reputation as a hard school, and I thought my resolve should be tested,' he said. 'Either you bend under pressure or you respond to the challenge. I can be very lazy and complacent unless I'm pushed so I knew I'd be weeded out very quickly if I was making a mistake.'

Study was six days a week and covered all the aspects of acting, from psychology of movement to the Stanislavski mix of 'Russian emotional freedom and Jewish introspection'.

It was, he admits, 'very unconventional in English terms. It was very much motivated by the extraordinary personalities of the men who ran it; they were hugely charismatic and very powerful, and rather frightening teachers. It certainly galvanized a lot of us into taking our energies to a different level.'

One tutor, Yat Malmgren, had himself been a student

of Rudolf Laban, who had revolutionized dance teaching by formalizing its notation. Yat translated his teachings into acting, using it to explain movement. 'We studied movement psychology and its notation,' Colin told actors' mag *Backstage West*. 'We didn't use the notation particularly, but the notation is based on principles of putting psychological concepts into space, into action, into the physical world.

'It all sounds terribly alienating and full of shit, really, to people who don't subscribe to it. I found that after a couple of years of it, it started to make an enormous amount of sense; it came as close as anything anybody really can to teaching acting. I think it's very hard to teach acting. You certainly can't teach talent. It made sense to me, and I still use it.'

And Colin certainly had talent. Unlike many of his schoolteachers, his tutors recognized his abilities and gave him leading roles in many of the centre's productions, including Molière's *Tartuffe* and Shakespeare's *King Lear*.

'As a boy and a young man, Colin was a person of conspicuous intelligence. Real intelligence,' said Christopher Fettes in a statement that might have surprised Colin's old headmaster. 'It is very rare to have the privilege of training people for the theatre who are by nature poets. And Colin is.' None the less, the exacting tutor wasn't going to give the golden boy an easy ride. 'It was an incredibly vigorous process, where you'd get rather pleased with yourself about what you were doing, and he would challenge you. He would give you cowardice,' recalls Colin. 'He would tell you to throw it all away.' On one occasion, after weeks of rehearsal, the student actor was convinced the dark spin he had put on the lead in *Tartuffe* was going to blow his audience away. Christopher instructed him to start all over again and come back the following Monday with a completely different approach. 'It was a torturous weekend. I just risked a completely different physicality. He was a healthy dose of a mixture of fear and respect that he engendered. He still has it over people even now.'

Away from classes, Colin was living the typical student lifestyle, hanging out in friends' flats and drinking cheap booze. But even now he found his middle-class background was getting in the way of his fitting in with some of his trendier peers. 'The inverted snobbery was very aspirant, the alternative culture was riding high and I wanted to be a part of that. But my street cred certainly wasn't going to be competing with the kids in that class: I wasn't a smack addict and didn't develop a criminal record.'

He still flirted with the idea of a rock star lifestyle and, like many creative teenagers, fantasized about a hedonistic way of life and a downward spiral into self-destruction. His own sanity and stable middle-class upbringing, coupled with the dedication to his future career, kept him from going off the rails.

'I romanticized the idea of artistically deranging oneself, whether it was a rock star fucking himself up with drugs or Rimbaud's conscious disordering of the senses,' he says. 'Being sane was a tedious, suburban thing to be. Unfortunately it's not the brilliance, but rather the screwing up, that's easy to achieve.'

His parents' habitual frugality had also stood him in good stead for student life. The meagre grant, he was finding, didn't stretch far in central London and he struggled to find enough money for food and lodgings.

'I've slept in railway stations,' he recalls. 'As a student, there was little pride and some grim places, grimy squats. It was just the sort of thing that students do.'

Choosing Nick Cave's 'Heart Attack Line' on *Desert Island Discs* in 2005, he said the track was reminiscent of his years in a student squat in Chalk Farm 'when one was quite happy to live in squalor.

'This was a period when I was homeless, not on the street but on other people's floors. You'd come home starving and try to find something in the fridge, and it wouldn't be there, so you check behind the sofa!'

Former acting coach Freda Kelsall was still in touch with Colin and remembers a visit to one grotty north London bedsit. 'I went to see him and he didn't have much money,' she said. 'He had holes in his shoes and was going to walk two miles to a play. But he was determined. I thought: "This boy is going somewhere."'

But it was a means to an end, and another turning point in the star's life. 'This is when I got my act together,' he says. 'To the immense relief of everyone around me, I suddenly wanted to do what was expected of me.'

Impressed with his good-looking protégé, who had cut his hair and adopted a less hippy look, Christopher Fettes paid Colin the ultimate compliment. If he could avoid being cast for his movie star looks, he said, he could become the next Paul Scofield. The comparison to his ultimate hero spurred Colin to work even harder. After years of teaching aspiring actors, Christopher had found his Hamlet and in Colin's final year he was cast in the lead role of his mentor's professional production. Colin disputes the general perception that the play was put on as a vehicle for him, although the college had never staged it before or since. 'He was engaged in a professional production of *Hamlet* and he had to teach us as well and it was more than he could do,' Colin concludes modestly.

Whatever the truth, Colin's troubled Dane was a sensation, described by one member of the audience as 'incredibly dark and glamorous'. And casting directors sat up and took notice. In early 1983 Colin was drafted in to play public school boy Guy Bennett in the West End production of Julian Mitchell's *Another Country* and he had some pretty big shoes to fill. Rupert Everett had made the role famous in its out-of-town run at Greenwich Theatre and had transferred to the West End with Kenneth Branagh playing the opposite role of Tommy Judd. When Colin was asked to audition, he was competing to replace Daniel Day-Lewis, but he wasn't the only one. The advert had been in *The Stage*, thousands had turned up and competition was stiff.

'There were guys dressed up,' he says. 'They tried to put the costume on, which doesn't sell, I don't think. And it's a really superbly bad idea; it's far too keen-looking. If you were to sit before the director and were a bit sceptical about your own chances for the role, they tended to like that. Anyway, I got past first base. It was a classic thing. I don't know if it happens any more, but it was the darkened auditorium and the light on the stage.'

Typically modest, however, he claims it was his looks that clinched the audition. 'Others were far better than me,' he says. 'But they weren't looking for a short fat guy with a slight Scandinavian accent. They wanted someone who walked and talked and looked like me.'

The play, loosely based on the life of Cambridge spy Guy Burgess, centres on the friendship of two public schoolboys. Guy is openly gay and Tommy is a Marxist. Both are shunned and despised by their peers and their masters. While public school was far from his own childhood environment, Colin immediately identified with both characters because of his experiences as an outsider. He accepted a salary of £150 a week and dropped out of drama school early. Even so, he was surprised that casting directors were already seeing him as one of the English upper-class set. 'To my astonishment I was identified immediately as silver-spooned, plummy.'

Lifelong friend Kenneth Branagh remembers the buzz around the play and the succession of brilliant actors who made their name in it, including Colin.

'When I was just about to leave *Another Country*, which was the first play I'd done when I was twenty-one, I remember coming in at the end of the run and downstairs rehearsing were Daniel Day-Lewis and Colin Firth, who was getting ready to take over,' he says. 'Also we used to go for a drink after the show with Gary Oldman, who was in a play next door, and Tim Roth, who was across the street in a play. It was one of those moments when you aware of a whole group of actors who were all starting at the same time and really going places so it's pretty nice when you bump into them these days, and we're still here, as it were.'

The play won Colin rave reviews and resulted in a moody poster of his young, good-looking face being plastered all over London. 'To me, it felt like megastardom,' he said. 'I made no distinction between that and a Hollywood role. I'd only been in London three years.'

Another Country launched the careers of Branagh, Everett and Day-Lewis as well as future Merchant Ivory star James Wilby. Colin couldn't believe his luck. With his first West End role came an agent and an Equity card, crucial for an acting career but incredibly hard to obtain. There also came the feeling that he had taken the right path, after all, and the happy knowledge that he had already shown his family that he could follow it through. 'That fairy godmother never appears again. It dwarfs what *Pride and Prejudice* felt like. I went from nobody knowing who I was and everyone doubting me to my dad taking photos of the poster on Finsbury Avenue.'

Indeed David couldn't have been more proud and was, no doubt, a little relieved. 'We never dreamt he would be straight on to the West End stage. It was about rebels against the system, so it was quite appropriate. Seeing him on stage was amazing, but the thing that made the biggest impact was going down the road past the Shaftesbury Theatre and seeing his portrait, huge, outside.'

As he was heading straight to the West End stage, in a leading role, without finishing his course, his peers naturally assumed he would soon be getting too big for his boots. But, as he has demonstrated to great effect ever since, Colin is resolutely down to earth. 'In the end I bought the drinks for a long time,' he says. 'I had to be humble.'

Others' perception of him did concern him, however. 'For a while I felt I had to be excessively modest so people didn't think I was above them,' he admitted to *The Guardian* in 1996. 'I forgot to return a phone call and now it was because I was thought arrogant, not because I was scatty and always had been. Then I realized nothing had changed. I was working, that's all there was to it.'

Two months into the run, Colin had another extraordinary stroke of luck. Director Marek Kanievska was planning a movie based on the Mitchell play and had cast Rupert Everett, the original Guy Bennett, in the lead role. The obvious choice for Tommy Judd might have been Kenneth Branagh, whose West End performance in the play had won prestigious awards, but his career had taken off and he was busy in Australia filming *Boy in the Bush*. Legend has it that Colin was asked to do a screen test in his place and that Marek was suitably impressed. Kenneth has a different recollection. 'The issue may have been that I wasn't available but I couldn't tell you whether they didn't just want Colin anyway,' he insists. 'I was in Australia doing the television series and to be honest I don't know the truth of that but he did a fantastic job in the film. Of course, I'd have been thrilled to do it but he was great.'

Whatever the truth behind the casting choice, Colin considered himself lucky to be landing his first film role so early in his career. 'I never even expected to work,' he recalls. 'When I left, I'd have been euphoric to get a spear-carrier in repertory. Films seemed like another world.'

With only his second acting job, Colin was about to become a film star. While he had cause for celebration, he sometimes seemed less euphoric than confused. 'I don't know what to expect next because I've lost my bearings,' he said during the filming of the movie. 'My sense of ambition has been numbed completely. When I got the part in the film, I already had a job and I didn't know how to react. On stage, you function on adrenalin, but the medium of film is very bizarre. The energy is different because the work is so detailed, so subtle. All I know is that I have to cope with what comes next in a very sober way and give myself a breathing space to sort things out.'

Some six years later he reflected that this wonderful opportunity had terrified him at the time. 'I wasn't nearly as concerned about the change of roles as the change in medium,' he said. 'It was not knowing if there was anything specific I should be doing that was so frightening.'

And co-star Rupert wasn't about to make the experience any easier.

CHAPTER 4

Toffs and Tiffs

I N JULY 1983 filming began on the film version of *Another Country* at Apethorpe Hall in Northamptonshire and various locations in and around Oxfordshire. Some scenes were also filmed at Earl Spencer's family seat of Althorp House, whose sumptuous rooms provided many of the interior shots. Although uncredited, Princess Diana's brother, Charles Spencer, can be spotted briefly by eagle-eyed moviegoers in a scene where the schoolboys sing the patriotic hymn 'I vow to thee my country', a line of which provides the film's title.

Moving the action to the big screen meant the glamour of the garden parties and stately homes could be better contrasted with harsher interiors of the boarding school's locker rooms, and the whole story gained a glossier, more photogenic look. It also moved the love story between Bennett and fellow pupil Harcourt, played by Cary Elwes, from off stage to centre stage.

While surrounded by genuine public schoolboys, such as Rupert and his old Etonian pal Piers Flint-Shipman, credited in the film under the name Frederick Alexander, Colin held his own on screen, with his clipped upper-class tones and boyish good looks making a real impact. Off camera, however, he wasn't fitting in quite so well.

Having been part of the process at its outset, and surrounded by friends who had worked with him since the play's first outing in Greenwich, Rupert Everett was keen to stamp his authority on the set and was soon ruling the roost. Unfortunately for Colin, the flamboyant star took against him, labelling him 'ghastly' and 'boring'.

In his autobiography, *Red Carpets and Banana Skins*, public schoolboy Everett admitted that he had initially fancied his co-star but he and Piers, who played Jim Menzies in the play and film, soon dismissed Colin as a 'grim *Guardian* reader in sandals'.

'He produced a guitar and began to sing protest songs between scenes,' wrote Rupert. '"There are limits," said my friend Piers Flint-Shipman when "Lemon Tree, Very Pretty" began. Colin was visibly pained by our superficiality.'

Secondary-modern kid Colin, who came from a very different background to the pair, was an earnest, politically minded young man at the other end of the scale from the frivolous attention-seeking star. 'Colin was very red-brick university, strumming a guitar,' Everett recalls. 'I remember him saying once that if he earned any money he was going to give it to the Communist party or something like that, and I was way in the other direction. He wasn't really much fun. We were at the end of the working-class revolution in the theatre at that time, that *Look Back in Anger* generation. English theatre was still very politically motivated when I started out, and it attracted a very politically motivated type of person. Colin was the kind of emblem for Redgraveism, and I didn't fit into that and I didn't like that whole Royal Court, RSC kind of right-on "kill 'em with art" vibe.'

Colin has since disputed Rupert's version of events, claiming he never wore sandals and that he doesn't remember bringing a guitar on to set either. Certainly, he says, he never learned to play the 1960s folk song, which compares love to the pretty but bitter fruit of the lemon tree.

'I did bring a copy of *The Guardian*, so I suppose the essence of Rupert's version is sort of true,' he told the *Sunday Telegraph*. 'It was a grisly experience – he was so badly behaved, and had the most powerful bullying technique, which was that he shimmied on to the set, and everyone promptly fell in love with him, so it was awful to be subsequently excluded by him.

'One was very easily seduced by Rupert. And he was much more worldly than me – I thought I was sophisticated, until I met him.'

And Rupert concedes that his youthful self was less than charitable to the inexperienced Hampshire lad. 'I'm sure I was just as nightmarish as he was, you know,' he has said. 'And *Another Country* was kind of my gig – I'd done the play, the producers were my friends, and I was probably a bit cocky in those days, you know, especially towards Colin.'

Colin agrees that 'Rupert got on with very few people. He found us all ghastly, naive and bourgeois.' But he admits there were faults on both sides. 'Basically I was unbelievably dull. And Rupert, well, among his virtues was not tolerance of earnestly dull people, so it wasn't exactly a marriage made in heaven at that time. We were both ghastly in our different ways.'

Rupert's obvious disdain made the set an uncomfortable place for Colin, and the Russian spy drama sparked a cold war between the two rising stars that would last for nearly twenty years. But the dynamic between them worked well on screen. The disaffected schoolboys of the film, although friends, are wildly different characters. Guy is a flamboyant, pleasure-seeking extrovert who enjoys the privileges his upbringing affords and is hungry for more. Tommy Judd, closer to Colin's personality at the time, is an intense, banner-waving Marxist who sees the public school and its hierarchy as a 'system of oppression'.

Contrary to popular belief, Judd is not based entirely on Guy Burgess's friend and accomplice Donald MacLean, but on an amalgam of one Esmond Reilly, a Wellington School boy whose left-wing magazine was banned, and John Carnford, a Communist killed in the Spanish Civil War.

Judd is ridiculed and ostracized for his views, and Colin admired the character's conviction to his cause. 'I'd never have Judd's strength in terms of allowing himself to become a joke in order to publicize his convictions,' he said. 'The way he sticks by these convictions all the time makes him unique. Most people don't have that kind of courage. They prefer to go along with the crowd.'

While sharing the earnestness of Judd, Colin claimed he was more in the mould of Bennett when it came to his own reaction against perceived injustices in the system and Montgomery of Alamein.

'Kids from middle-class families were slotted into academic pursuits while those from less literate backgrounds did carpentry. I wasn't a Communist, and when I rebelled against those assumptions, it was more as Bennett would have done. I was scruffy, I was cocky and I was trouble, but I didn't go around voicing principles.'

As well as launching Colin on to the film scene, *Another Country* afforded him a taste of the high life to come. The film premiered at the Cannes Film Festival in May 1984 and won the coveted award for the Best Artistic Contribution. At twenty-four, Colin was walking down the red carpet at one of the most prestigious events in the film calendar and being fêted by all those around him. Everyone except, of course, Rupert. The leading man, claimed Colin later, refused to speak at the press conference for the movie because of his co-star's presence.

While it was his first foray into the trappings of stardom, the young actor didn't exactly shrug off his earnest image with his reaction. While his hedonistic and well-connected co-star was, no doubt, enjoying the parties and people that Cannes's famous Croisette offers festival-goers, Colin took the luxuries bestowed on him with a large pinch of salt.

'It's a shock how quickly you take things for granted,' he said. 'How after three days of limousines, big dinners and photographs in Cannes, it stops being interesting. I certainly feel that as an actor, you have to ask yourself every day why the hell you do it.'

Although he later admitted that sudden fame 'blew me away', Colin appeared sanguine about his uncertain future at the time and ready to roll with the punches. He had expected to pay his dues on leaving drama school and work his way up from the walk-on part, and his dream had been to start his own theatre company, but *Another Country* had already lifted him to another dimension and he confessed, rather plaintively, that 'I've lost my bearings'.

'My sense of ambition has been numbed completely,' he said. 'When I got the part in the film, I already had a job to be shameful emotions,' he said. 'I think it's important to reflect them. I think also that the story about the bloke who's absolutely fine isn't really a story. And so the further you can go with the problems the more the story is there. It's not really a question of how fucked up I can make this person. It's more to do with how high I can make the stakes. How big can I make the obstacles? I do believe the drama is more interesting if the obstacles are bigger.'

From there, he moved on to the TV adaptation of Terence Rattigan's *The Deep Blue Sea* to play a former RAF pilot whose passionate affair with a married woman leads to the end of her marriage. When the philandering flying ace loses interest in his desperate lover, played by Penelope Wilton, she attempts to commit suicide.

A small part in *A Circle of Friends* reunited Colin with Pat O'Connor, his director from *A Month in the Country*, and his *Chatsky* co-star Minnie Driver. Set in Ireland, it's the gentle tale of a group of young students in the fifties and Colin played the arrogant son of a wealthy landowner who beds the bewitching Nan Mahon, played by Saffron Burrows, leaving her pregnant and leading to her tricking another man, played by Chris O'Donnell, into marriage.

In the role of Simon Westward, Colin got to brush up on his horse-riding skills and his seduction technique. Both were to come in handy for the life-changing role that was about to come his way.

CHAPTER 8

The Darcy Dilemma

WHEN PRODUCER SUE Birtwistle finally got the green light to film a new adaptation of *Pride and Prejudice*, after eight years working on the project, she already had her Mr Darcy in mind. She had worked with Colin Firth on *Dutch Girls* some ten years before and her husband, Richard Eyre, had directed him in *Tumbledown*. Sue was convinced that he had all the qualities needed to play the smouldering, taciturn landowner – but it seems she was the only one who was.

'I knew he'd be perfect. But no one agreed with me – least of all Colin Firth himself!' she told *The Guardian*. 'He thought Jane Austen was just girly stuff and didn't want to do a classic drama. He didn't know Darcy was such a famous character in English literature and was amazed at people's reactions when he said he was considering the part – comments like wasn't Darcy supposed to be sexy and Olivier played it and he couldn't do it better.'

Having finally convinced the bigwigs at the BBC, Sue was heartbroken to receive a call from Colin saying he couldn't see himself in Darcy's riding breeches and he was off to LA any minute. In fact, he was seriously considering the very different role of a drag queen in the movie version of *Priscilla Queen of the Desert*.

'I was cast down in gloom,' recalled Sue. 'I wrote a long letter and couriered it and the script to Colin, urging him to read it on the plane. I waited a whole day in agony, with my fingers crossed, hoping that he would read it and reconsider. Finally he phoned – and claimed his part.'

All six scripts arrived on his doorstep at a time when he was sick of reading bad scripts and felt he really didn't want to plough through another one for a drama he wasn't keen on. 'Everything seemed unreadable, and so the last thing I thought I needed was six episodes of a BBC costume drama against which I had a prejudice,' he said later. 'I was casting my mind back to the 1970s, when it was the last thing in the world I watched on television. I remembered it as stiff – stiff acting, stiff adaptations.'

Colin opened the envelope with some trepidation. During his teen years lost in Sartre and Camus, he had avoided reading the standard school texts of Austen and assumed them to be 'girls' stuff'. Still finding his feet in the film industry, he was also loath to commit himself to a project which would tie him to the UK for six months. By page 4 of Andrew Davies's imaginative and sensual dramatization, however, he was hooked.

'It was remarkable,' he recalled in Sue's book *The Making of Pride and Prejudice*. 'I didn't want to go out until it was finished. I don't think any script has ever fired me up so much, just in the basic romantic story terms.'

Even so, Colin was hesitant. While he had fallen in love with the story, he was having a great deal of trouble imagining himself as the leading man. He remembered one theatre review, which had cruelly asserted that 'Colin Firth doesn't have enough romantic charisma to light a 50-watt bulb'. He asked family and friends and they were little help. Brother Jonathan's incredulous, 'Darcy? Isn't he supposed to be sexy?' was not the only off-putting remark. Others harked back to Laurence Olivier's performance in the 1940 film opposite Greer Garson, and told him 'no one else could ever play the part'. Colin also pointed out that the book is written from Elizabeth's point of view and therefore Darcy remains an enigma until the end and it is difficult to play a part that is based on everyone else's image of him. 'The only way to do it is to be Darcy already. I looked in the mirror and I didn't see Darcy.'

In the end it was Sue Birtwistle's unerring faith that he was the only man for the job that swayed him. After a meeting, in which she inadvertently revealed the ending before he'd had a chance to read the final episode, he reread the whole thing and thought some more. 'I agonized and imagined myself doing it, and then tested the notion of not doing it and it occurred to me that I would feel rather bereaved if I turned it down.'

As an established actor, Colin was not asked to do a screen test or audition. Having taken the decision to sign on the dotted line, the next step was the read-through, where he would meet his co-stars. Jennifer Ehle had been chosen from a wealth of hopefuls to play his love interest, Elizabeth Bennet, Alison Steadman would play her mother, Mrs Bennet, while the dainty shoes of her four sisters would be played by Susannah Harker, Julia Sawalha, Lucy Briers and

Above: Colin (front row, centre) attended Barton Peveril College near Winchester from 1977 to 1979, where he learned to love acting and determined to study at the Drama Centre in London.

Right: It wasn't long before his talent and good looks were noticed by casting directors, and in 1984 he played Tommy Judd in Marek Kanievska's movie based on Julian Mitchell's play *Another Country*, opposite Rupert Everett as Guy Burgess.

Above: His first part in a costume drama was as Armand opposite the beautiful Greta Scacchi in the TV adaptation of Alexander Dumas's *Camille*.

Above: In 1985 Colin played public schoolboy Neil Truelove in the TV movie *Dutch Girls*, alongside Timothy Spall.

Above: The TV adaptation of J. B. Priestley's *Lost Empires* was an extraordinary experience for the young actor, as he played opposite greats such as Sir Laurence Olivier.

Below: In *A Month in the Country*, Colin played opposite Kenneth Brannagh. By now firm friends, they had first met while in the stage version of *Another Country*.

Above: His role in *Valmont*, an adaptation of the French novel *Les Liaisons Dangereuses*, was important as he honed the many skills – fencing, dancing, riding – that he would later use in the role of Mr Darcy, but also because of his off-screen romance with co-star Meg Tilly.

Left: Colin and Meg fell in love, eventually deciding to 'disappear' together. They lived for two years in the wilds of British Columbia, three hours from Vancouver in Canada, where, in September 1990, they had a son, William.

Right: In summer 1991 Colin flew back to London to star in a run of Harold Pinter's *The Caretaker* at the Comedy Theatre, opposite Donald Pleasance.

Above: And then came *Pride and Prejudice* … The role that
made Colin Firth a household favourite, as Mister Fitzwilliam
Darcy, opposite Jennifer Ehle as Miss Elizabeth Bennet.

Above: In *Fever Pitch* in 1997 Colin swapped tight breeches for Arsenal colours in his portrayal of obsessive football fan Paul.

Above: As The Earl of Wessex in John Madden's *Shakespeare in Love*, a low-budget British movie that managed to bag seven Academy Awards in 1998.

Above: By the turn of the millennium Colin Firth had a tremendous fan base and was able to turn his hand to drama and comedy.

Left: With his sister, voice coach Kate Firth, who was to help Colin master the stammer he needed for his role as King George VI in *The King's Speech*.

Right: Colin with his proud parents, David and Shirley at the premiere of *Hope Springs* in 2003.

Left: Videoing his son, William, at the Chinawhite Cartier Polo Party in Windsor Great Park in 2002.

When writing the novel *Bridget Jones's Diary*, author Helen Fielding always had only one man in mind to play Bridget's real love interest, 'Mark Darcy', in the film version … *Above:* Colin with Renée Zellweger and Hugh Grant at the premiere of *Bridget Jones's Diary* (2001); *right,* a tender moment in *Bridget Jones: The Edge of Reason* (2004).

Polly Maberly. The entire cast gathered in the BBC rehearsal rooms two weeks before filming and most, including Colin, were wracked with nerves.

Crispin Bonham Carter, who was cast as Darcy's friend Charles Bingley, recalled going into the gents' toilets and finding Colin 'groaning aloud in agony, which was no help at all'. Consummate professional Alison Steadman soon put everyone at ease by launching into a spirited performance as the common but ambitious harridan Mrs Bennet. This broke the ice between the assembled company, who rounded off the evening with chilled white wine and nibbles, as they got further acquainted. A week's rehearsal followed, at the insistence of director Simon Langton, where any glitches in the script could be ironed out and the first scenes to be shot were gone through. As the shoot is out of order, Darcy would be declaring his love for Elizabeth before the scene when they met was shot.

'There was definitely a lot of pressure on us,' he told *The Independent*. 'It was a five-month shoot and that was in the third week. It was one of the first major dialogue scenes we had to do. It was very intimidating for that reason, and I spent the weekend doing a hell of a lot of homework on that particular scene just before we did it. I remember people trying to take the pressure off it. They were going round saying, "Don't worry about Scene 47. It's just like any other. Just treat it like any old scene." Of course it all made it worse.'

Before filming began, Darcy's look had to be perfect and make-up designer Caroline Noble admits her first reaction to Colin was dismay. Whereas the Jane Austen hero is dark and brooding, he turned up with fair hair, cut short, and a moustache he had grown for another part. 'I think I actually said, "Oh God!" Because I was surprised,' said Caroline.

'Simon thought he'd arrived "looking like an unmade bed". But Colin was open to all suggestions.' At their request, he allowed his naturally curly hair to grown out in the weeks leading up to filming and it was then dyed a dark brown. His eyebrows and lashes were also dyed to complete the look. The dark look was accentuated by the deep greens and grey of the costume and the early sketches of the outline show the riding breeches and knee-length boots that would come to define the character.

Five months of filming began in a field in Grantham in June. As the character of Fitzwilliam Darcy is often away attending to business in the Austen novel, Colin had big breaks between his stints on the shoot, a fact that unsettled him. Although he was the leading man, the story revolves very much around the five Bennet girls and their mother's attempts to marry them off, and Colin admits that his old feelings of being an outsider crept in. 'I came down to location and all these other people were there, whom I didn't know at all, doing another film which seemed to be about a family of girls . . . It did interfere tremendously, I think, with my sense of being part of it.'

He did form a tight bond with some of his male co-stars over a shared love of music. During the evenings together, when raffles, quiz nights and boules competitions kept the cast amused, Adrian Lukis, David Bamber and Colin would bring out their guitars and practise long into the night.

Filming took place in several rural counties, including Warwickshire, Oxfordshire, Wiltshire and Buckinghamshire. For Netherfield, the home of Charles Bingley, who falls for Elizabeth's older sister Jane, Edgecote Hall in Banbury was chosen. The beautiful stately home of Lyme Park in Cheshire doubled as Darcy's palatial home. Due to a change of management, however, only exterior shots could be shot there and the interiors of his home were filmed at Sudbury Hall in Derbyshire and Lacock Abbey in Wiltshire. This not only created a split shoot, meaning the cast and crew had to travel between the two locations, sometimes to finish the same scene, but it also meant that, if the weather turned, it wasn't so easy to switch to shooting interior shots instead.

The country house of Lyme Park was built in the 1720s and nestles in a deer park of 1,359 acres on the Derbyshire–Cheshire border. Now owned by the National Trust, it was chosen as the perfect home for Darcy because, as a man on 'ten thousand a year', he would have the most impressive estate. It was here that the famous lake scene, which sees Darcy emerge in his dripping shirt after taking a dip, was filmed.

When the scene was broadcast, the nation's women went into a collective swoon. But Colin later revealed that it should have been even saucier – and the original script called for him to swim naked. 'Originally I was supposed to take all my clothes off and jump into the pool naked,' Colin revealed to *The Observer* in 2000. 'The moment where the man is a man, instead of a stuffed shirt. He's riding on a sweaty horse, and then he's at one with the elements. But the BBC wasn't going to allow nudity, so an alternative had to be found.' At one point there was talk of underpants but that was judged historically inaccurate. 'He would never have worn underpants. They would have looked ridiculous anyway.' Finally, after several meetings, it was decided that, rather than strip off, he should jump in almost fully clothed.

For Colin, the decision was a relief as he admits to 'a bit of the usual tension about getting your kit off'. He also believes, as many a female viewer would no doubt agree, that it is a sexy image because 'we rerobed, not disrobed, Austen'.

Shooting the scene when the soaking-wet hero bumps into the object of his desire and exchanges a few bashful words, director Simon Langton had inadvertently created TV gold. 'Nobody had the slightest inkling that Colin Firth, wearing a lightweight cotton voile shirt with his nipples showing underneath, would have such an effect,' he said.

Almost a year later, the broadcast of that impromptu swim would propel Colin from a small fan base to an international sex symbol. And yet he was as blissfully ignorant as his director when it came to its potential impact. 'For some reason it became a huge event, even though there was nothing in the way the scene was shot or scripted that anyone had the slightest suspicion would be seen as sexy,' he said. 'And then of course I found myself being waved at and followed down the street in London!'

Ironically, the thirty-four-year-old didn't actually take the plunge in his most memorable scene. Simon also revealed, some years later, that the swimmer was in fact a stuntman as there were fears over the cleanliness of the lake water. Insurance clauses prevented the actor diving in and the underwater shots were actually filmed in a tank in Ealing Studios. 'We didn't want our leading man to catch Weil's disease, which can be caught from rat urine in water,' he admitted.

Colin's dip in the studio tank didn't go quite as planned either. 'I hit my nose so hard on a steel girder at the end of the tank that we couldn't film the next day,' he said. 'With so much gushing blood and swelling, nobody was thinking, "This is really going to get them going."'

If Colin didn't make a splash, his portrayal of Darcy certainly did. The series proved the biggest drama hit for decades and the final episode went out to over 10 million viewers. Britain's latest sex symbol had pulses racing all over the country, including one woman who Colin was told was taken to hospital with high blood pressure and told not to watch any more of the series. She was 103.

'It's a testament to the contortions of viewers' imagination that that scene is remembered the way it is because I read stuff about the wet shirt clinging to these chiselled contours,' he said later. 'And I didn't have chiselled contours!'

On set, the dashing Darcy had conquered another heart – that of co-star Jennifer Ehle. Gorgeous, glamorous and single, the pair had been thrown together for five months filming the most romantic story of all time and the inevitable happened. They fell in love.

'People fall in love with the people they meet,' Colin later explained. 'It's as simple as that. I don't think that actors have a greater predilection for bonking each other than any other group. I just think that your life is in upheaval. You're taken away from your established roots and put in intimate circumstances with someone. I suppose it makes that sort of thing more possible. It certainly doesn't happen to me all the time.'

Insiders on the set claimed that the air of romance was palpable during filming of the last episode, when Elizabeth and Darcy finally kiss. They tell of 'bruised lips and sexual tension' as the scene was shot, time and time again, to get it just right.

Colin dismissed the reports and said the scene was shot in one take. 'We were losing the light. There was no giggling. Why would we giggle? No, we were involved with each other, but it's perfectly simple to do a chaste little matrimonial kiss.'

By the time the on-screen love story hit the living rooms

of the nation, however, the off-screen romance was over. The discreet couple had managed to keep it under wraps during filming but, with Darcy mania reaching epidemic proportions, the secret was discovered by the press long after the event.

'We were together for almost a year,' said Jennifer later and, referring to the attention that the pair received after the broadcast, she added, 'It was a blessing that our relationship ended before the show was aired.'

Colin later insisted that the closeness of a shoot, especially one which takes up six months of your life, is bound to lead to on-set relationships. 'There's this absurd perception that actors are fucking each other all the time,' he said. 'But it's just that you tend to end up with the people you work with.'

Jennifer also felt the on-screen passion contributed to the couple's attraction to each other. 'Being on location and acting in a story opposite somebody is incredibly conducive to falling in love,' she told *Tatler*. 'If you took two people who work in a bank and who might possibly fancy each other if they thought about it, and you make them stand there saying "I love you" every morning, really trying to mean it, eventually they might, you know, start to believe it.'

Having signed up for a TV series and a film, which together would mean months in Italy, Tunisia and South America, Colin was facing another long-distance love affair and the practicalities soon got in the way. The relationship floundered and the lovers went their separate ways. Clearly burned by the experience, Jennifer swore off dating fellow actors. 'It's so hard to have a relationship in this business,' she said. 'I don't want to do it again unless it's unavoidable. It's just not worth it.'

As with Meg, however, there was no animosity and they parted on friendly terms.

'Colin is a very nice guy and a great actor,' Jennifer told the *Daily Mirror* in 2002. 'He's been good in everything I've seen, whether it's *Shakespeare in Love* or *Bridget Jones's Diary*. By the time *Pride and Prejudice* came out, we were not a couple. The way our so-called "affair" was reported was so wrong. We were two single people in a proper relationship which ended.'

It was strange, she added, that a publicity photo taken in the *Blue Peter* garden at the BBC studio in Shepherd's Bush, on the day of the read-through, was published after the event, 'like some sort of engagement photograph'.

Two years later in 1997, Colin decided to put the record straight about the romance. 'It wasn't at all a brief fling,' he told *The Times*. 'I've never mentioned this to any member of the press but I don't see why I shouldn't now, just to clear it up. It was written about as a brief location fling. Jennifer Ehle and I were together for almost a year. I had known her for a few years a little bit and the relationship began when we were working together and lasted until, well, it was all over by the time *Pride and Prejudice* came out.'

Pride and Prejudice was aired in the UK from 24 September 1995, when Colin was away filming *The English Patient* in Italy. Blissfully unaware of the huge impact his simmering alter ego was having, he was only home for one week during its six-week transmission and was astonished to find giggling women were stopping him in the streets. His agents, who had been largely unmolested by his fans in the past, were fielding thirty or forty calls a day from women wanting to know what he would star in next and whether they could see him at the theatre. Fan sites were being set up on the Web, and in Suffolk extra security had to be laid on to stop panting ladies stroking the doe-skin trousers that Darcy had soaked in his most famous scene. The mere mention of Colin's name in female company was guaranteed to illicit a lovelorn sigh. He had become a bona fide sex symbol. And nobody was more shocked than he was. His new status was, he insisted, 'the most improbable thing ever to happen to me as an actor. People would have howled with laughter if I'd tried to predict it. In fact, they did when it first happened.'

The modest actor, who admits he had been surprised to be asked to play the romantic lead at the age of thirty-four, was not always comfortable with his sudden popularity. But he was grateful it hadn't come at an earlier age, when he might have fallen into the trap of believing his own publicity.

'If this had come up early in my career, say when I started out at twenty-three, it would have been confusing and I would have had a very distorted image of myself and my strength as an actor,' he said. 'But I don't look for male hunk roles. I think that can be tedious both to play and to watch.'

The BBC adaptation became the biggest costume drama success story in the corporation's history. Penguin couldn't reprint the classic novel quick enough to supply the demand and the first batch of BBC videos, some 12,000 copies, sold out in two hours.

'We put it all down to the appeal of Darcy,' said a BBC spokeswoman. 'There's no other reasoning for it. Episode four was the killer. I've never seen an actor so consistently wet.' Hysteria was reaching boiling point. 'We've had people in tears, ringing us for copies. One woman called us crying yesterday because she couldn't get a copy and she was going on holiday. She was desperate to see it before she went.'

Colin admitted that, despite his relationship with Jennifer, he had felt immune to the romance of the period drama and the ladies' heaving bosoms. He told the *Radio*

Times, 'it wasn't my cup of tea' and added, 'I felt like a drug dealer who doesn't get high on his own supply. I'll peddle the stuff but won't use it. All I did was put on a costume and act.'

In 1996 the series was nominated for six BAFTAs, including Best Actor for Colin. On the night it was only Jennifer who picked up an award, for Best Actress, but the public attention stayed firmly focused on her leading man.

'I don't resent that he gained more notoriety than I from *Pride and Prejudice*,' Jennifer later revealed. 'I feel fortunate that I got to play Elizabeth Bennet in a good adaptation and got to escape the popularity and notoriety. I just hope that, with all the sex symbol stuff, people don't forget what a damn good actor he is.'

Proud dad David enjoyed his son's performance in the drama and was amused by the viewers' reaction to the taciturn, moody landowner. Colin, he confirmed, couldn't be less like the character. 'I think people are quite shocked when they meet him,' he told the *Daily Mirror* in 2001. 'They expect him to be like Darcy, but he is quite an excitable person who likes larking around. He's very noisy – the life and soul of the party. He's a very dominant personality. He doesn't get recognized much, because he doesn't look like Darcy in his own clothes. But he was in a play in London and a group of American women arrived to see it. They had travelled all that way to see him.'

Ever the realist, Colin reasoned that the legion of women who had taken him to their hearts were not really lusting after him personally. 'I enjoyed the recognition in some ways, but it was as if my whole career came down to that one part,' he said. 'It wasn't really me that everyone was crazy about – it was the character.'

Back home in Hackney, he insisted, his neighbours

couldn't have cared less about his new-found idol status. 'Nobody gave a shit,' he recalled. 'It meant I could go out in my pyjamas to pick up the Sunday papers and the bog roll, and nobody would comment. I didn't fancy getting dressed to do those things. In fact, I still hate getting dressed.'

The Darcy tag propelled him to the A-list but, although it was fun to bask in the limelight for a while, it was also to prove something of a millstone around his neck for the next fifteen years. Even when he chose varied roles, as far from the nineteenth-century romantic hero as possible, the spectre of Darcy was to haunt him at every turn.

CHAPTER 9

True Romance

SOON AFTER FILMING wrapped on *Pride and Prejudice* Colin prepared to fly out to South America to film another BBC drama, a £10 million production of *Nostromo*. Leaving his relationship with co-star Jennifer Ehle behind him, the thirty-four-year-old actor was about to meet the love of his life.

The notoriously difficult Joseph Conrad novel is the story of Englishman Charles Gould, who inherits a silver mine in the fictional South American country Costaguana. As war threatens his livelihood, he enlists the help of a journalist and the eponymous hero Nostromo, an Italian sailor, to smuggle out his silver. When their ship is attacked by rebels, the treasure goes missing and only Nostromo knows its whereabouts.

Financed by a conglomerate of British, Spanish and Italian backers, the shoot was an international affair. Serena Scott Thomas played Gould's wife, Italian Claudio Amendola took the title role and 15,000 Arhauco Indians stood in as extras. Filming in the stifling heat of Colombia took its toll on cast and crew alike and director Alastair Reid ended up in hospital after losing consciousness on set.

Struggling into his period costume while being filmed for a video diary, Colin stoically quipped, 'You have to have a masochistic delight in sweating and suffering. The Brits love this stuff more than anybody. It is the Italians and the Spanish who complain about it.'

Other actors made his life uncomfortable too. Although he had spent much of the Austen shoot on horseback, and ridden in *Valmont,* he found it daunting to be controlling a steed on the noisier set, with a mock civil war raging behind him.'You'd be sitting on a horse that wasn't really trained in front of fifty to a hundred other horses and carriages on a dirt street in a shantytown with the camera miles away and a huge crowd and a language barrier and explosives going off,' he explained. 'They gave me a quite uncontrollable horse the first day, a mustang or something, and I was thrown for the first time in my life – and I pride myself on being quite good . . .'

In another scene, Colin's character is being garrotted and he had a metal collar around his neck. Not understanding the instruction yelled at him, Colin was nearly strangled for real and, because of the language barrier, was unable to tell his Spanish co-star to stop.

A few weeks into the shoot, the Italian contingent were joined by a stunning twenty-six-year-old production assistant called Livia Giuggioli, working while on a break from studying at a university in Rome. 'I was having a slightly miserable time and we'd four months to go, and she showed up,' he said. It was love at first sight. 'I immediately felt she was amazing, and it was very quick,' he recalled. 'It was instinctive, inexplicable, and I've never looked back. She is an Italian beauty and the smartest woman on the planet.'

Colin described the moment the couple met as being like a lightning bolt. Before he even spoke to her, he sensed a special connection. 'We met in Colombia, in Cartegena, which is a staggeringly beautiful city full of staggeringly beautiful people', he told Ellen DeGeneres. 'I was on the steps of a church, a very old church in the plaza, and that was it – it was a bolt to the heart.'

The feeling was so sudden that Colin was frozen to the spot, too nervous to walk over and chat. 'I didn't move. I couldn't move. And I realized with trepidation that she was coming closer and I'd almost hoped she wouldn't come my way because I couldn't cope. But she just came over and shook hands and she had this completely guileless air about her. She just shook hands and tried to speak to everyone in their own language and I was smitten. She dates it from that moment too, when we actually shook hands.'

By the time filming finished, the couple were deeply in love and splitting their time between her home in Rome and his flat in Hackney. But at twenty-six, Livia still lived with her parents and Colin had to put in some groundwork to be accepted into the family. 'Because of the conventions of her family, being Italian, my courtship with my wife was quite formal and very old-fashioned,' Colin explains. 'And I think our relationship benefited from that.'

Fifteen years later, when he received the Best Actor gong at the Venice Film Festival for *A Single Man*, he paid tribute to her family for taking him 'on trust' and recalled the obstacles he had to overcome to win their approval. 'I'd shown up as this very, very dodgy commodity, attached to their darling daughter,' he told *The Sunday Times*. 'When we got together, she told them, "I've got this English chap now"– one strike against me. "He's an actor"– hmmm, oh, dear. "He's nearly ten years older"– oh, boy. "And he's got a kid with someone else." I had a mountain to climb to win everyone over.'

A few months into the relationship, however, the full force of Darcy mania hit in the UK and, overnight, Livia became the most envied woman in the world.

'The poor girl met me before the Darcy thing happened and she hadn't heard of me,' he told *The Observer*. 'She is Italian and my name doesn't mean squat in Italy. She just thought she had a fairly normal boyfriend and all that stuff happened.'

As the nation's women went wild for Colin, he hid in Rome, where he could stay fairly anonymous and avoid the constant references to his wet breeches and clinging white shirt. He did attempt to impress his potential in-laws with his female following but they remained unmoved. 'I mentioned, half jokingly, that I was something of a sex god in England,' he recalls. 'They both burst out laughing!'

Hearing the buzz about their daughter's boyfriend from England, however, they were intrigued enough to arrange a night out at the cinema to catch one of his movies. The only thing playing at the time was *Circle of Friends* – not exactly the movie to prove his point. 'Appealing in that I am not,' he admits. 'They were in despair at this ghastly, bloated, moustachioed English fool. Then, when they were sent tapes of *Pride and Prejudice*, there was a general kind of disbelief that anyone could find this man sexy.'

Even Livia's friends were amazed by the British reaction to the repressed and emotionally stunted Darcy. Having watched the drama with Livia, one of her closest pals remarked ask incredulously, 'Do the English find this sexy? Do they also find John Major sexy?' Livia, meanwhile, found the frenzy over her English boyfriend hilarious.

Another old acquaintance who was shocked by the sex symbol tag was Jennifer Tilly, the actress sister of Colin's ex Meg. 'I was on a chat show when they announced the next guest as "England's new sex god, Colin Firth". I couldn't believe it,' she laughed. 'When you know someone as your sister's boyfriend, it's hard to see them as a heart-throb.'

Even Colin couldn't really believe what he was hearing about Darcy mania, until mum Shirley sent him a recording of a radio discussion on the subject. 'I thought, "Christ! This has never happened before, this is extraordinary."'

• • •

As the nation swooned over Mr Darcy, Colin was off on his travels once more. Having filmed a few scenes for *The English Patient* in Italy, a happy coincidence for courting couple Colin and Livia, he flew to the deserts of Tunisia for a nine-week stint. With journalists clamouring for interviews, and posters being pinned up in offices all over the country, his 'tendency to withdraw' once more kicked in and, refusing all requests, he was relieved to have an excuse to escape. 'All this sudden attention threw me,' he admitted. 'I thought I knew where I was professionally. I didn't think this was on the cards.'

The cuckolded husband of Katharine Clifton, played by Kristen Scott Thomas, couldn't have been further from the romantic hero of the BBC series and was a comparatively small role. But the screenplay by the late Anthony Minghella, who was also directing, was immensely promising and Colin was keen to be involved.

The film, based on a Booker Prize-winning novel by Michael Ondaatje, centres on a badly burned Second World War pilot, Ralph Fiennes, in the care of a young nurse, played by Juliette Binoche. Through a series of flashbacks, his doomed love affair with the married Katharine Clifton is revealed, as is his true identity. When her betrayed husband, played by Colin, finds out about their relationship, he exacts a terrible revenge.

Colin arrived in Tunisia in November 1995, at the height of Darcy fever, much to amusement of his co-stars. Screen wife Kristen told *The Times*, with a playful swoon, 'I'm acting with the new heart-throb of England: Colin Firth. Darcy. He's my husband. If you're not convinced he's a complete heart-throb, the rest of England is. They're even doing Darcy clubs. People visit the house where it was filmed to look at the pond where he emerged in that wet shirt.' Joking, she added, 'It's all make-up, you know.'

Acclaimed director Anthony Minghella was proud of his company for the movie and thrilled to have the new 'heart-throb' on board. 'Colin's an exceptional actor, one of the best of his generation,' he said. 'Like Ralph he's a highly intelligent and adroit player and has in common with him an emotional rigour.'

For Colin's role as deceived husband Geoffrey, he drew on his past feelings of exclusion, the sense that he was the only one left out of a private joke. 'I was very much the outsider in that film. It seemed that what was really going on was between the others. I could be doing all the talking, but it was all about the glances between my wife and this other bloke, and I eventually lose her to Ralph Fiennes. I am never going to let that happen again.'

In a pivotal scene in the movie, Geoffrey returns to the

hotel where he is staying with Katharine, to collect something he has forgotten, and sees her leaving for an assignation. As she spends a passionate evening with her lover, he sits in a cab outside the hotel all night, awaiting her return. 'Nothing happens, but it's a tremendous scene, because you're very sympathetic to Kristen, but Colin keeps pulling the point of view around to him,' commented Anthony. 'He brings a gravitas to a character who could be something of a buffoon.'

Having moved around a lot in his childhood, Colin's had always had a sense of rootlessness and his chosen profession had made his adult life equally nomadic. But as his romance with Livia grew stronger, he was beginning to crave a little more stability. And after two months in the sweltering heat of North Africa, filming in Tunis, Al Mahdia and Sfax and the desert environment of Tozeur, Colin was showing signs of settling down. 'Wherever I am, people always say, "You're always away,"' he complained. 'You feel like the invisible man. I'm never here, I'm never there. So where am I?'

But his relationship with the Italian beauty, who was still finishing her doctorate in English literature, meant that when he wasn't filming he now had three bases – London, Rome and LA, where he spent time with his young son.

Will, now six, was at school in LA and Colin spent as much time as possible visiting him. The pain of separation from the lad was often intense but Colin didn't feel that, in splitting with Meg, he had abandoned his son. 'I don't consider I have left him,' he told *The Times*. 'I go away a lot, and I come back a lot. Of course, I wouldn't be seeing enough of him unless it was every day. And there are risks. There's a danger you become a sort of Santa Claus. You have to find enough normality as well – to give a child the chance to be bored with you, take you for granted and feel it's safe sometimes to reject you. I think about that a lot.'

In the wake of *Pride and Prejudice*, which had proved a hit in the States, Hollywood had once again thrown open its doors and even Steven Spielberg put in a call. Colin agreed to meet with the legendary director out of curiosity and flew over to LA to see him. 'It was weird to find that someone who is such an enormous figure in the business was so chatty and informal and unassuming. He had his feet up, and was wearing a baseball cap and sipping a McDonald's Coke.' Exciting though it was to meet the man behind the biggest blockbusters of all time, Colin wryly reported, 'He didn't invite me to do his films.'

Colin was surprised at the impact the role was having on his profile. 'Although before it, I thought I was extremely successful,' he joked, 'it wasn't until afterwards that I realized that no one had noticed me.'

Typically, with LA calling, Colin's response was to run as fast as he could in the opposite direction. After several multimillion-dollar contracts failed to raise his interest, he signed up to play middle-class football fan in *Fever Pitch*, at a fraction of the fee.

'I was chased for big movie parts after playing Mr Darcy but they didn't interest me,' he told the *Daily Mirror*. 'I am not comfortable in costume drama and some scripts were simply an excuse to get me back into tight breeches.'

TV offers were also on the table, but Colin shied away from the long-term commitments required. 'The offers weren't all abominable,' he said. 'But even if they weren't, there would always be a little detail like, "Just sign here and don't worry because it probably won't happen but if this goes to a series, you're with us for ten years". It was very Faustian.'

The low-budget British film Colin chose is based on a

best-selling autobiographical book by Nick Hornby but for the screenplay the author became the fictional character of Paul. Despite the public image of Colin the posh, privileged type, the part of the obsessive Arsenal fan was closer to his own reality than any of the aristocratic parts he had played.

'There's a tremendous amount of the character, Paul, in me, which I think is eventually true of most people I play, although I admit his cultural background is a bit closer to mine than Darcy's.' In the wake of the Austen hero he was desperate to do something at the other end of the spectrum and was happy to turn down the potential riches of the US market to prove he could be something altogether different. 'It's more fun being Nick Hornby,' he insisted.

The decision to play an ordinary, modern-day Arsenal supporter didn't win immediate approval from fans of football or Firth. Letters to newspapers asked why he was doing a football film when he could be playing Heathcliff in *Wuthering Heights* while Arsenal fans asked why this 'snooty geezer' was playing one of them. 'I somehow feel I'll be pleasing nobody now,' he lamented.

But he was determined to challenge the stereotype of the typical supporter and strike a balance that would show both sides of the story.

'There's this idea that if you like football, you also like beer and grabbing women's breasts,' he said to *The Times*. 'If you like rugby, you also like Dire Straits and wine. And if you don't like either, you must be a pacifist vegetarian who is oblivious to the charms of Michelle Pfeiffer.'

The screenplay touched a raw nerve in Colin's soul and took him back to his teenage years, when his attempts at gaining some sort of street cred were scuppered by his middle-class background in a respectable suburban family.

'I'm a secondary-modern-educated white suburban male,' he told *Intelligent Life* magazine. 'Nick was the same generation and grew up in Maidenhead, which is exactly like where I grew up, and what really resonated was this idea that boys from the suburbs don't have any roots. You step out of school and into a cultural void. There's no music from your part of the world that makes you want to weep into your beer. There's been no artistic revolution or sacrifice. One ends up casting around for credentials of some kind, claiming some sort of Celtic blood, yearning to be a Delta bluesman – or in Nick's case, Charlie George. I may be English, but my sensibilities reside in Rome. I may be middle class, but my granny comes from Brum. Anything just to give yourself a bit of substance.'

Colin was in Rome with Livia when he first read *Fever Pitch* and, once again, the thought of settling down crossed his mind. 'It gave me a yearning for England and the sort of rootedness that Nick Hornby talks about – the kind of rootedness you have to find, because it is not something you grew up with . . . I felt he wrote about Englishness now – my generation – in an extremely unsentimental and yet not hostile or bitter way. And I found that quite unusual.'

Contemplating the transient nature of film-making, he sounded more and more wistful about putting down roots. 'Making a film is so self-contained that very little else enters your consciousness,' he told *The Times*. 'Then it's over, and the chances are that you will never again see people who have become your entire existence. A certain amount of consistency is essential to anyone, and I have found it difficult being without that as time goes on.'

While Colin was running from the Darcy image, co-star Ruth Gemmell could hardly get the famous wet breeches out her mind. When signing up as Paul's girlfriend Sarah in the

As the millennium celebrations approached, he seized the opportunity to make the nation giggle once more by accepting a brilliantly funny cameo in Rowan Atkinson's *Blackadder: Back and Forth*. While he missed out on the lead in *Shakespeare in Love*, he got to play the Bard in the time-travelling comedy, which was filmed as a one-off special for screening at the Millennium Dome in Greenwich.

Running into William Shakespeare in a corridor, Blackadder makes him drop a sheaf of papers which the viewer can see is a draft of *Macbeth*. After asking for an autograph, Blackadder sends him sprawling with a punch in the face before telling him, 'That is for every schoolboy and schoolgirl for the next four hundred years!' He then berates him for condemning future generations to 'hours spent at school desks trying to find one joke in *A Midsummer Night's Dream*' and 'Years wearing stupid tights in school plays and saying things like "What ho, my lord" and "Oh, look, here comes Othello, talking total crap as usual."'

He then kicks Shakespeare and adds, '. . . that is for Ken Branagh's endless uncut four-hour version of *Hamlet*'.

The tiny role marks Colin's first collaboration with writer Richard Curtis, who would later put words in the mouth of his character in *Love Actually* and be instrumental in his next big movie role, in *Bridget Jones's Diary*.

The busy year of 1999 wrapped up with the Boxing Day screening of *The Turn of the Screw* on ITV. The spooky ghost story, adapted from a classic Henry James novel, is set in a country house where the charismatic master, played by Colin, employs a governess to look after his two children. The new arrival (Jodhi May) soon begins to see two mysterious figures, which the housekeeper informs her are spectres of a former governess and valet, who are both dead.

'I love the mystery of it,' Colin told the *News of the World*. 'When ghost stories are told well, they are brilliant. But they are incredibly rare. It is a perpetually misjudged form of storytelling. I also like the mood of a ghost story. It is perfect for a cold wintry night, sitting by the fire. In fact, perfect for Christmas.'

The down-to-earth actor revealed he didn't believe in the supernatural but admitted to some 'uncanny and inexplicable' experiences in his past. 'When I was a teenager I dreamed up all sorts of things, but as I got older I've found explanations for them all.'

The one ghost that Colin was haunted by was Mr Darcy, and he was aware that taking another period drama role always risked stirring it up once more. 'Let's just say I'm not a fan of this kind of production,' he stated. 'Despite my reputation for it, I am not drawn towards watching period drama on television. But on the other hand, I won't steer away from it just because Darcy was so successful.'

His role as the romantic hero's namesake, Mark Darcy, in *Bridget Jones's Diary* was to be Colin's final attempt to lay that ghost to rest.

CHAPTER 12

Darcy Revisited

EVER SINCE THE iconic pond scene in *Pride and Prejudice*, London's most famous fictional singleton, Bridget Jones, had been lusting after Colin in print. When her best-selling book looked set to make it to the big screen, author Helen Fielding had only one man in mind to play Bridget's real love interest, the starchy but sensitive lawyer she had named after the Jane Austen hero.

'I had just finished watching the miniseries *Pride and Prejudice*, and, like most of London, I fell in love with his Mr Darcy,' she explained. 'As a wink, I named Bridget's "Mr Right" Mark Darcy. I described him to look like Colin Firth. In fact, part of me was worried that the actor would feel my descriptions were too close to him.

'In my wildest dreams, I never thought he would actually play Darcy in the movie. But a girl can dream.'

Colin had taken a fair amount of ribbing from his friends and family over Bridget's lustful diary entries and at first he had refused to read them. Curiosity got the better of him, however, when the mention of his name got more frequent and he began to read regularly. 'It was a hall-of-mirrors thing for me. Very bizarre.'

Before he was asked to star in the celluloid version of *Bridget Jones's Diary* the search was on for the perfect Chardonnay-swilling, weight-obsessed thirty-something to take the lead role. *Titanic* star Kate Winslet was favourite for the role but turned it down when the production took too long to get off the ground, leading to clashing schedules. Producer Eric Fellner voiced his disappointment in February 2000, saying, 'We were in negotiations for the deal. I am absolutely amazed that it didn't work with Kate.'

Helen Fielding was keen to cast an unknown in the role, believing an ordinary girl would be more believable as Bridget than a glamorous star. 'I keep seeing girls who I think would be perfect for the role,' she revealed. 'My favourite was a girl in the gym who was sitting on a machine reading a magazine and not exercising at all. I nearly walked up and offered her the part.'

The final casting was a surprise to everyone. Renée Zellweger was a super-slim thirty-year-old Hollywood star with a Texan drawl – a far cry from the chain-smoking, calorie-counting Sloane. But she was a big fan of Helen Fielding's original book. 'The diary is an amazing evocation of the life of a single girl. It reads like Jane Austen, with comic and ironic twists and turns,' she said.

Before perfecting her accent, Renée had to wean herself off her habitual lifestyle of low-fat healthy food and regular exercise. The *Jerry Maguire* star tucked into pizza, peanut butter sandwiches and fast food in a bid to gain weight. 'I've put on more than 15 lb and I'm very proud,' she said, just before filming started in the summer. 'I'm down to three pairs of sweatpants and four T-shirts that still fit. Everything else is in boxes ready to be shipped home.'

In order to immerse herself in British culture, she also rented a flat in Kensington, listened to the Spice Girls, and went to work in a London magazine office. 'British women are less hard on each other and less judgemental than Americans,' she told the *Sunday Express*. 'I suppose it's because they're not judged as harshly themselves. When it was somebody's birthday, everybody had a piece of cake. In LA, nobody would have eaten it.'

With Renée on board, the producers were free to approach their first choice for Mark Darcy. Colin had been expecting the call and had already mulled it over in his head. This, he thought, would bring his association with Darcy full circle and prove that he could poke fun at his own image. 'There's a certain inevitability about it,' he said. 'I think it's healthy for me to do it.'

Hugh Grant was cast as Mark's love rival, the dashing cad Daniel Cleaver, and Jim Broadbent was on board as Bridget's long-suffering dad. In another bizarre life-imitating-art twist, the film was to be directed by Sharon Maguire, the model for Bridget's best pal Shazza in the column and Helen's real-life best friend. And Andrew Davies, the man who had Colin making a splash in *Pride and Prejudice*, was one of the writers called in to tweak the script.

Colin had become an avid reader of the column but took issue with Bridget's division of friends into either singletons or smug-marrieds. 'I'm married and extremely content. Extremely happy. But I don't see the world in terms of married and single people. I would never walk into a dinner and be horrified that they were all couples except me.'

He told the column's home paper, *The Independent*, 'There are certain things that I didn't identify with – weight and boyfriends – but I did think it was very funny and I think the script's very funny as well. I wouldn't be doing it if I didn't. And it's got a very good cast. I wouldn't have done it just to be symmetrical about the Darcy thing.'

While embracing the connection between the two Darcys, he still sought to distance himself from the BBC series that had propelled him to heart-throb status. 'I don't have anything to do with anything I did six years ago,' he said. 'I don't know if you remember how you spent your summer of '94, but that's how I spent my summer of '94, and that's about it.'

However, as he prepared for the role of 'v. eligible bachelor' Mark, he did watch some of the scenes again partly, he said, to inform his performance. 'I'm not playing Mr Darcy but I am aware there's a reference involved and I was just curious again to see if I could understand what the fuss was about.'

He admitted that the series told 'an intoxicating story', told with beautiful language and that the actors 'did a good job'. But he insisted that the focus should have been on Jennifer Ehle's performance as Elizabeth Bennet, pointing out that she was the one who walked away with the BAFTA. 'Darcy is the romantic destiny. She's the one you're meant to identify with.'

Although the two Darcys are from different eras, Helen Fielding and screenwriters Andrew Davies and Richard Curtis had given Mark many of his namesake's character traits and had even recreated scenes from the 1995 hit drama.

In both productions the hero is at a social gathering and 'standing there looking down his nose at everyone', Colin pointed out. 'And it reminds me of high-school parties where you'd stand there, feeling all hung up and repressed. And the only way you can deal with that is to pretend it's because you're superior and enigmatic. So that's what you hide behind to deal with the paralysing situations.'

The fact that the social paralyses are misinterpreted as smouldering superiority is what appealed to Colin. He finds it hard to be consciously sexy, 'But if a director says, "Be really revolting and a bit dull", you think, "Yes, I can do that, I manage that every day."'

Although playing with his image of the taciturn, brooding love interest, Colin remained uncomfortable with his sex symbol status and modestly claimed he wasn't even sure he was attractive.

'I am considered attractive by some people and I've been completely ignored by others, so I know that I am somewhere in the middle,' he told one journalist.

Asked by yet another whether he considers himself attractive, he answered, 'Does anyone? I have good days and bad days. I don't recall ever looking in the mirror and having a fully fledged erotic experience. I've tended to try and put it down to a combination of things; playing a role, having the right make-up, and the cameraman being very generous.'

But he also claimed the reaction to his most famous role stripped him of his identity. 'I felt as if I'd lost my whole personality,' he told *The Observer*. 'It's been very strange, this idea of Mr Darcy appealing so much to women. Because obviously, as you can see, I don't carry that around with me. I'm not Mr Darcy every day of my life. If people expect to see a saturnine, dark, smouldering tall aristocrat, they are going to be disappointed.'

Having been constantly reminded of his wet-shirted

hero and the effect he had on the opposite sex, Colin decided, 'I might as well have some fun with it and join in the process.' But he confessed that the two productions had taught him nothing about the opposite sex, saying that back in 1994 'I knew nothing at all about women. And I still know nothing about them.'

Unlike the famous Mr Darcy, Mark was required to shed his shirt in *Bridget Jones's Diary* so, while Renée was fattening up, Colin was vowing to get in shape. 'I was threatened with the prospect of having to take my shirt off, which was a chilling thought,' he recalled. 'So I decided that, rather than change profession, I'd get a trainer and try to do something about it.'

The trainer in question was Cornel Chin, whose previous claim to fame had been getting Leonardo DiCaprio fit for his swimwear in *The Beach*. Called in two weeks before filming, Cornel had Colin on a strict diet of pasta, poultry, fish, cereal and rice, with no alcohol or fried foods.

'Colin wanted to meet a target in a short time so we had to work incredibly hard,' he said. 'We blitzed his whole body. He is one of the most hard-working clients I've had.' The star's daily workout was ninety minutes long, beginning with a fifteen-minute warm-up jog and a series of aerobic exercises plus 400 sit-ups. Colin lost a stone and gained an impressive six-pack.

'Colin has done exceptionally well,' Cornel marvelled. 'There's a distinct difference and I don't think his female fans are going to be disappointed. Now he is in really good shape. He is a lot leaner than he was as Mr Darcy, when he was fairly podgy. He has lost a lot of weight and it shows. He has made a complete lifestyle change.'

Delighted with his new buff look, Colin vowed to keep

up the good work. 'I definitely needed to get in shape for the film. In this day and age you need to be in trim if you are going to be a top actor,' he confirmed. 'But I wanted to get in shape regardless of the film, and this is going to be a lifelong commitment. To get fit for the role was a bonus, but I intend to stay in shape for life now.'

Five years later he was still sticking to his promise, and going for regular runs. On *Desert Island Discs* in 2005, Sue Lawley asked him if he felt there was 'a fat person inside trying to get out'.

'There certainly is, and he's doing ever better as time goes on,' replied Colin. 'Until I was thirty I was one of those people that stayed slim. In fact I was so thin I wouldn't even go to a swimming pool when I was twenty, and it seems impossible to get fat. But these days I have to go for a run if I want to stay this shape.'

Part of the reason for his fitness regime was a fight scene with Hugh Grant. *Bridget Jones's Diary* was the first time that Colin had worked with Hugh, who at the time was Britain's biggest box office draw. Both articulate and quick-witted, the pair entered into a playful rivalry on set that became a running banter away from the shoot.

'Hugh's been telling everyone that I fight like a girl,' joked Colin after shooting the scene. 'All I can say in response is that it takes one to know one! He was the first one to pull my hair – I'd never have dreamed of doing that. And he scratches as well, so that should give you an idea of his character.'

In truth, Colin has a great admiration for his intensely funny co-star. 'He is the best actor of light comedy that we have, the best actor of light comedy anywhere,' Colin told *The Times*. 'Light comedy implies something less substantial than drama but that's quite untrue. What Hugh has is an extremely inaccessible ability. I can think of very few actors at all since Cary Grant who have had it but there are millions of talented dramatic actors.'

As a true gentleman, Colin defended the casting of his American co-star Renée by telling everyone that she had the British accent spot on. And he revealed that she didn't drop the London twang once, even when the cameras stopped rolling. She is, he told journalists, 'a gem to work with. She's generous, friendly, professional and sounds like she comes from north London.

'I've never heard a peep of the Texan accent out of her yet, so I've got to know her as this person who comes from down the road. And it's actually a little bit confusing sometimes because there's a great incongruity when she tells you something about her childhood in Texas. She says something like "Dad lassoing mustangs and taking me to the rodeo". And you think, "What, in Croydon?"'

Some time after the movie wrapped, Colin bumped into Renée in an LA hotel and stopped for a chat. 'She's now wandering around using what I think is a rather unconvincing Texas accent,' he cheekily reported.

Remembering his own experiences on an American movie set, Colin felt protective of Renée. 'I've been in that situation too, in *A Thousand Acres*, where I had to be an American in front of American actors. It is mortifying.'

With the role of Mark Darcy being taken by Colin, the question arose of the sequel, should there be one. As the second book, *The Edge of Reason*, contained the now famous interview between Bridget and Colin Firth, who would play Colin?

'You might have to change the character of the actor,' he suggested when the matter was broached. 'Someone the

Americans believe is a credible sex symbol!'

As filming wrapped at the end of the summer, Colin was contemplating his upcoming fortieth birthday. 'I feel like a bizarre genetic experiment that's gone wrong,' he joked. 'It's all happened far too quickly.'

While he was keen to leave behind the more obvious romantic leads and seek out character parts, he was aware that he would soon be ruled out of some desirable projects on the grounds of age alone. He related a telling anecdote about an actor friend who shared his agent going up for a role that Colin would have liked in the previous year. His agent informed him that he wasn't in the running because the character was in his twenties. When he protested that his pal was thirty-five, his agent agreed but pointed out, bluntly, that Colin was thirty-eight. 'Suddenly I realized that it wasn't a lot between us, but I was on the other side of a fairly important barrier as far as casting is concerned,' he told *The Times*. To make matters worse, he revealed, the agent then rang him back to tell him the part had been offered to his brother Jonathan, who was six years younger.

With three years of marriage under his belt, and his fortieth looming, Colin was also thinking about starting a family with Livia. Again, he was feeling the passing of time and, having felt too young to fully embrace the huge responsibility of children when Will had been born, he was determined not to feel too old when any subsequent children arrived.

'It'll happen,' he said and, on the subject of leaving it too late, he added, 'There does seem to be very little in between. You finally reach adulthood and you go through a time of being too young for everything – I'm not thinking about acting here. "Oh, you've got plenty of time, it's all in front of you, you'll find out that later in life," and then suddenly on a dime you're past it, you're not young any more. There does seem to be a missing middle bit.'

By the time his fortieth arrived, on 10 September 2000, the couple had made a start on their next big production. Livia was three months pregnant.

CHAPTER 13

Pride and Parentage

AFTER THE PURE fun of *Bridget Jones*, Colin moved on to his darkest role to date. *Conspiracy* was a truly chilling dramatization of a meeting which sealed the fate of six million Jews.

On 20 January 1942, fifteen senior Nazis met in a villa at the lakeside village of Wannsee, on the outskirts of Berlin. Over a buffet lunch, followed by coffee and brandy, they coolly discussed the 'Jewish problem' and after ninety minutes of talk came up with the infamous 'Final Solution'.

After the meeting Adolf Eichmann produced thirty copies of a transcript, only one of which survived the war. The terrifying dialogue based on this document has the Nazis casually discussing the extermination, sterilization and forced emigration of the Jewish population of all the European regions under German control and those they intend to conquer.

Colin's character, Doctor Wilhelm Stuckart, was the

legal mind behind the Nuremberg laws. At the gathering, he made a particularly disturbing speech which begins with his sounding as if he abhors the mistreatment of Jews, because he argues that the SS view that they are subhuman is wrong. But he finishes by proposing a solution that is almost as inhumane as the gas chambers. Urging his colleagues to face 'the reality of the Jews', he tells them, 'To kill them casually without regard to the law martyrs them and it's their victory. Sterilization recognizes them as part of our species but prevents them becoming part of our race.'

The star-studded cast was led by Kenneth Branagh, as SS officer Reinhard Heydrich, and included Ian McNeice, David Threlfall and Stanley Tucci, who played Adolf Eichmann. Devoid of frills such as background music and camera tricks, the content alone was powerful enough to make a huge impact on viewers.

'It is shattering stuff,' Colin explained on set. 'This is utterly banal. They cracked a few jokes. Discussed whether bullets were better than gas. Whether sterilization was better than forced emigration. Basically, the brief was no messing around with these half measures. We have to free German living space, as they put it, from all Jews so there is not one left.'

The clinking of glasses as the extermination of Jewish men, women and children is casually debated emphasized the pure disregard for human suffering. 'He talks about it as if it were a meeting to discuss foot and mouth disease,' Colin told *The Daily Telegraph*. 'That's what's astonishing: these men cracking jokes, passing the cheese, looking at their watches . . . and talking about genocide. I think what is shocking is how you can get reeled in. Put yourself in that position: could you be one of the men round the table?'

For human rights campaigner Colin, the horrific discussion was both historical and contemporary. Hitler may have been defeated, he argued, but similar war crimes were still being perpetrated. As the TV drama was filmed in London and Germany, Serbians were being tried for their part in the ethnic cleansing programmes in the former Yugoslavia.

'I am reading a book on Rwanda at the moment,' he said. 'And it is remarkable to me how many parallels there are. The Balkans might be a more fitting comparison.'

The Germans at that fateful lunch, he observed, 'weren't doing it in the spirit of passion, but because they felt it was necessary and that their lives would not be better until they got rid of an entire race of people. The same sort to normalization of what is absolutely unthinkable is still happening today.'

Paradoxically, the horrifying content of the script led to a certain amount of levity on set, at least initially. Colin remembers the first few weeks of filming were punctuated by fits of giggles.

Firth, last seen parodying his doppelgänger Mr Darcy in *Bridget Jones's Diary*, immersed himself in Holocaust literature for the part and found himself haunted by the experience. Yet the first month of filming was marked by fits of the giggles.

'That could be quite hard for people to understand, and possibly offensive,' he told *The Sunday Times*. 'When you put fifteen boys together and introduce something that makes them all a bit nervous, it's a recipe for slightly hilarious ribaldry, although we weren't joking about the subject matter.'

In the initial read-through, the actors were torn between their horror and the need to lighten the mood, meaning they laughed at the chilling gags in the script and then covered their mouths in disgust. 'It was when they were discussing how to sterilize people without them knowing. Someone said you could have an X-ray machine hidden under a desk. At which, another character says, "I'm not coming into your office."'

The true evil behind the meeting hit home when the cast travelled to Berlin to shoot scenes at the actual villa in Wannsee where the meeting took place. The building is now a Holocaust museum and Colin, who had read numerous books on the genocide, was moved by the exhibits on show.

'I was born in 1960, and for those of us not directly affected, the Holocaust had seemed like ancient history,' he said. 'It had been difficult for me to maintain my outrage. But there were photographs in that museum – medical experiments, some involving children – which are some of the most horrific things I've ever seen. I was haunted for months afterwards.'

On its release the TV movie was widely acclaimed, winning a Best Actor Emmy for Kenneth Branagh and Best Supporting Actor nod for Colin. It also won Best Single Drama at the 2002 BAFTAs and Stanley Tucci took the Best Supporting Actor at the Golden Globes.

• • •

Before filming the hard-hitting drama, Colin embarked on a new venture for pal Nick Hornby, in agreeing to write a short story for publication. *Speaking with the Angel* was a collection of tales by various writers, including Irvine Welsh, Helen Fielding and Robert Harris, in a fund-raising tome for the Treehouse Trust, a charity which runs schools for autistic children, one of which Nick's son Danny attended. Colin, who had always harboured a secret desire to write, was honoured to be included among the talented authors, but he confessed he found submitting 'The Department of Nothing' harder than taking on a film role. 'Writing has not been a deadly serious secret pursuit before launching myself on the world. It's a hobby I enjoy – something I might do in Biro on an aeroplane,' he revealed. 'But it is a lot more exposing than I imagined.'

His first-hand tale of a prepubescent lad who lives a fantasy life through his bedridden grandmother's daily storytelling session was well written and moving. The lad's isolation at school echoed Colin's own schooldays, and his temporary popularity, brought about by his repetition of Gran's episodic adventures, mirrored a status he would have wished for in secondary school but only truly achieved after finding his acting talent.

'When I agreed, I thought, "I'm an actor, I'll just ramble on until I find a voice," but it just kept coming out awful,' he told *The Sunday Times*. But he admitted he was 'chuffed' with the finished story.

At home, as Livia's pregnancy progressed, Colin was being more attentive than ever. With the March due date looming, she decided to leave London for Rome in order to be closer to her parents when the time came and because, he later joked, 'My wife preferred to suffer in Italian.' Her husband happily agreed, knowing that it would mean she was safe in the bosom of her family, should the baby arrive when he was away for work or promotion for the soon-to-be-released *Bridget Jones's Diary*. It also meant that the press failed to get wind of the impending birth until the very last minute.

'I'm absolutely over the moon. It's about to pop, and no one has sussed it,' he told *The Guardian* in March. 'Ever since

I met Livy, people have been speculating that she's pregnant and it's never been true. Now she's enormous and she's been in public but, weirdly, people stopped pursuing it.'

When the stars turned out to London's Leicester Square for the glitzy premiere of *Bridget Jones's Diary* on 4 April 2001, Colin, minus his wife, walked down the carpet wearing the biggest grin of them all. Just days before, on 29 March, Livia had given birth to Luca. Colin had been at the birth and had cut the umbilical cord, which he described to *Vogue* as 'an unbelievable experience. Friends of mine who had been through the birth of a child warned me that there could be relationship problems afterward, because in your mind you have a picture of your wife in pain. However, I found the whole process from conception, pregnancy and birth to be an erotic experience. For me it was an erotic cycle that culminated with the birth of a child.'

Despite the fact he was 'walking on air' at the premiere, it proved a wrench to leave Livia so soon after the birth to attend the event in London and then, a week later, another in LA. But at least his language skills were benefiting.

'My Italian is pretty good but I'm adding words like "burp" and "wipe" to my vocabulary,' he admitted at the US junket. 'I spoke to him on the phone this morning and he burped. I was in tears.'

In an afterthought, which may well have come back to haunt him later, he compared his new son to a root vegetable. 'He looks a little like a turnip,' he joked. 'But a beautiful turnip.'

Having had plenty of practice on his oldest son, Will, in the wilds of Canada, changing nappies came naturally and he is a very hands-on dad. Being older the second time around was also a great help because, he revealed, 'this time,

Above: At the Toronto International Film Festival in 2003.

Below: Colin with the late Natasha Richardson and her husband Liam Neeson at the premiere of *Love Actually* in 2003.

Above: With his wife, Livia Guiggioli, at the film premiere of *The Importance of Being Earnest* in New York in 2002.

Below: With Emma Thompson and Bill Nighy, two of his co-stars in *Love Actually*. Colin was to work with Thompson again shortly afterwards in the highly successful *Nanny McPhee*.

Above: With Scarlett Johansson in the highly acclaimed film version of Tracy Chevalier's novel, *The Girl With the Pearl Earring*.

Above: In 2004 Colin embraced his darker side in *Trauma*, a bleak drama directed by Marc Evans. He said he found it a welcome relief from all the romantic comedy he'd been playing of late.

Left: In late 2004, Colin took part in a campaign for Oxfam, shot to promote the charity's Trade Justice Movement, which called for governments around the world to halt unfair trade practices.

Below: In another part of the same campaign, Colin is seen here with the then European Trade Commissioner, Peter Mandelson, handing over Oxfam's Big Noise petition at the EC headquarters in Brussels, December 2005.

Above: It was his old 'adversary' Rupert Everett who approached Colin to star as the starchy school inspector, Geoffrey Waites, in *St Trinian's*, the sixth film in the series of classic comedies. This was the first time they'd worked together since *Another Country* eighteen years previously.

Above: Colin with co-stars Amanda Seyfried, Meryl Streep and Stellan Skarsgård at a photocall for *Mamma Mia!* in 2008.

Below: Unfortunately the rom-com *The Accidental Husband*, in which Colin starred with Uma Thurman, wasn't well received by the critics.

Above: At the premiere of *A Single Man* with Tom Ford, who directed the film, and co-star Julianne Moore. Colin received a BAFTA for Best Actor and was nominated for an Academy Award for his role in this stylish movie.

Above: Colin with Helena Bonham Carter as the Duke and Duchess of York (later to become King George VI and Queen Elizabeth) in the multi-award winning international smash-hit *The King's Speech*.

Left: Geoffrey Rush (in background) played Australian speech therapist Lionel Logue in the film, which received widespread critical acclaim as well as breaking box-office records.

Right: Geoffrey Rush, who was also executive producer on *The King's Speech*, and Colin at the film's premiere in London in October 2010.

Left: Colin grips his Academy Award for Best Actor, a proud moment for him and his family.

Above: In January 2011 Colin received his star on the
Hollywood Walk of Fame, which is laid next to that of his
friend and sometime co-star Emma Thompson.

I feel a little more equipped for it'. Unlike Will's infancy, when he had been on a self-imposed career break, the success of *Bridget* had made him hot property once again and the offers were flooding in. Having always limited his work to maximize time with his eldest, Colin now had to factor in his second family when it came to picking projects. He was careful to strike a balance between work and home, stating that 'I am at the point where my family and spare time are more important'.

'I'll be a dad who goes to work,' he told *The Guardian*. 'I do intend to be a dad. If I do do something in the summer, it'll have to be something where I can have my kids around me.' The continuing adulation over Darcy, he said, 'pales into insignificance next to the things you really care about in your life'.

Thankfully, young Luca was a cooperative baby so Colin could turn up on set in the morning without the usual baggy-eyed look of the new dad. 'He must have Chianti in his blood,' he told Italian *Vogue*. 'We're lucky; he's slept through the night from the beginning. Everything gets taken care of for him except eating and sleeping.' And he joked that, as soon as he got to work, the roles were reversed. 'It's the same with actors. The actor finds himself in a childlike position. Someone tells you when to get up, you could actually turn up naked because someone at work will dress you anyway, they blow-dry your hair. Your face gets made up. Actually, it's miserable. Someone even tells you when you should eat. Then you are shown where to stand, what to say and how. Then in the evening, it's reversed.'

Warming to his theme, he continued, 'Why doesn't my wife appreciate it when I throw my dirty laundry on the floor? When I call my agent, he drops everything. I'm not a person with airs, but those are the rules of the industry. They dance around you like the Golden Calf.

'When you come home and you have a hungry baby that is crying, then you are the one that must let everything else go. You can't call your agent and say, "My children are behaving obnoxiously, do something to make them stop!"'

Bridget Jones's Diary opened on 15 April 2001 to rave reviews and a huge box office bonanza. With an opening weekend of £5 million in the UK and over $10 million in the States the movie had made most of its £16 million budget back within a few days and the final gross came in at £175 million ($280 million).

The critics on both sides of the Atlantic loved the film, and the new Mr Darcy, as much as the public did.

Stephen Hunter of the *Washington Post* wrote, 'Grant is casually fabulous and very amusing, but all power to Firth the actor. He's the compleat Darcy, and he never wavers . . . You can see him simmering with rage – at Bridget for being so attractive, at himself for never quite knowing what to say, at both of them for being prey to such childishness, at his libido for wanting and at his ego for fearing. Especially poignant are his long looks at her. You see in his eyes his yearning hunger and his fury at his own ineloquence and inability to find the will to move ahead, from across the unbridgeable distance of a large room filled with happy people.'

In the *Daily Mail* Christopher Tookey commented, in mock *Bridget Jones's Diary* style, 'Firth excellent at little eye-flickers that give away hidden sensitivity beneath,' and added, 'Also makes change to see articulate Englishman in movies who is not complete swine or twit.' And *Independent* critic Laura Tennant gushed, 'Firth might as well have "good husband material" tattooed across his forehead, but despite this, or perhaps because of it, he makes a devastatingly sexy Darcy. And ladies, I mean devastating.'

No sooner had Colin returned from the worldwide promotion of the movie, however, than he was on set for his next one. Fortunately, *The Importance of Being Earnest* was to be filmed in London's Ealing Studios and at West Wycombe Park, the home of the infamous upper-class miscreants The Hellfire Club, and for Colin a forty-five-minute drive from home. Costume fittings, conveniently, took place in Rome so the busy actor could spent plenty of time with Livia and Luca during the eight-week shoot. According to the producer, Barnaby Thompson, he and co-star Rupert Everett came away with seventeen outfits each, although Colin insisted, 'I never demanded them, I was provided with them!'

Although it had now been eighteen years since they fell out on the set of *Another Country*, the two leads had managed to avoid each other since. Having recently completed *An Ideal Husband* with *Earnest* director Oliver Parker, Rupert was the natural choice for this next Oscar Wilde classic. But he wasn't exactly chuffed when he learned who his co-star would be.

'I certainly had some trepidation,' he admitted. 'Later Colin asked me what my reaction was when I'd been told that he'd been offered the part of Jack. And quite honestly I said, "Oh God, not him again!"' Rupert added that he had been pleasantly surprised when Colin turned up at the read-through without his 'awful guitar' and told him he was glad he had 'lost that red-brick "Robin-Hoody" thing that you were working in the old days'.

Colin was less worried. The characters of Algernon and Jack are best friends and bitter rivals who spend the entire play throwing clever insults at the other. Oliver assured them that any 'frisson' would work in their favour.

'I was fascinated after all these years,' Colin told *The Times* in August 2002. 'I mean, even if we still couldn't stand each other, I thought, "That's got to be interesting, to see what happens this time." And I suppose in some ways I wondered if we were born to be a couple really. The dynamic is not that different now; it's become slightly more grotesque, and then it was slightly more elegant and we were younger and it had to do with political idealism.

'And it worked in *Another Country* because you had one character who is extremely intense and idealistic and another one who basically wants all the privileges of life and is flamboyant. And that reproduces itself, to some extent, in *The Importance of Being Earnest.*'

Colin still had one issue with Rupert. Standing at six foot two, Colin was used to being the taller one on set but his old adversary was six foot four and it made him feel unusually small.

'It's not often I'm looking up to someone and feeling like the little guy. But I swear Rupert's grown in eighteen years,' he continued. 'I feel like I'm Ernie to his Eric or something. Actually, it's even worse, I feel like Peter Glaze to his Leslie Crowther. You know, the little round angry man constantly frothing with the indignity of it all, that's me, and he's the tall, funny, languid fellow.'

Director Oliver was aware of the pair's past antipathy and was keen to make sure that it didn't make for an unhappy set when shooting began. He insisted on taking them both out for a pre-shoot dinner and he revealed he was pleased with the resulting truce.

'Actually, they are like brothers now,' he said to *The Times*. 'They are fantastic at bantering and bickering, it's really funny. Rupert is so sharp and Colin comes up and matches him.

And they were like that all the way through filming. I actually think they are extremely fond of each other.'

Wilde's most famous comedy has the young Jack Worthing living a double life, facilitated by the invention of a brother, Ernest. The imagined existence of the wayward sibling allows him to live the wild life in London without fear his misdeeds will be reported back to his seat in the country and, more importantly, to his innocent young niece, Cecily Cardew. Algernon uses a similar subterfuge to escape to the country. This tangled web of lies begins to unravel when Jack falls for Gwendolen, who believes he is Ernest, and Algernon attempts to woo Cecily, who believes the same of him.

Colin remembered watching the play in Southampton as a lad, and feeling rather inadequate when he failed to find it funny.

'I saw it as a teenager in a repertory theatre,' he recalled on the US *Today* show. 'It was rather a stiff production and in the way you normally see Oscar Wilde represented, which is actors composing their faces to look droll and playing to well-informed laughter. Actually, you're sitting there thinking, "I'm supposed to find this funny. If I'm smart, I find it funny." But you're sort of slightly shut out from it. When I read it, I howled with laughter. So I always felt there was a slight discrepancy.'

The cast for the film included Dame Judi Dench in the iconic role of Lady Bracknell, Tom Wilkinson, Anna Massey, Edward Fox and American star Reese Witherspoon, who was cast as Jack's young ward. Colin was drawn by the Wildean wit and the stellar company.

'You can't get better writing if you're looking for light comedy and it's pretty much a pinnacle of English wit,' he said on set. 'When you ask me what attracted me about this, it's irresistible. I can't imagine anybody saying no to an offer to be among these people. There isn't one person in the cast who isn't absolutely first rate, 100 per cent best at what they do. It's fantastic.'

Saying yes to the project did cost Colin one important date in his diary though. He had become a devoted fan of Arsenal since his turn in *Fever Pitch* and in May he was delighted that his beloved team made it through to the FA Cup Final. But the match was to be held in Cardiff's Millennium Stadium and Colin was required on set in London. 'Colin can't believe he is not able to attend the game – he loves Arsenal with a passion,' said his agent. 'But he has filming commitments in London. He is hoping to take a big break in the afternoon – starting at about 3 p.m.!'

On the day, the Gunners lost 2-1 to Liverpool, no doubt giving Rupert Everett plenty to rib Colin about on set. And the banter stepped up a notch when a scene called for them to serenade Cecily and Gwendolen – and Colin produced the reviled guitar.

'I did study the guitar part, hoping that some kind of ability on the guitar might make up for my vocal shortcomings,' Colin remarked. 'But I'm afraid it didn't.'

Visiting actress Reese let slip an insight into the relationship between Rupert and Colin at the film's New York premiere the following year. They had managed to get over their differences, she suggested, by bitching about everyone else. 'I already knew that Rupert Everett and Colin Firth are both renowned in the business for being catty,' she said. 'Their big game on set was always trying to get Dame Judi Dench involved in their bitching. They would start talking about people in the business, and continually ask her what she thought of them.' Dame Judi would not be easily drawn.

'She would put on this imperious voice and just say, "I'm not having anything to do with this at all."'

In later interviews, however, Colin claimed Reese was far more serious on set than the formidable Dame Judi. 'It may be shocking to some people, but a lot of the American actors I've worked with are far more disciplined than Judi Dench,' he said. 'Judi has a terrible sense of mischief, and sometimes you're lucky to get beyond three lines of dialogue without her cracking up with laughter. Of course, she's very sure of her own discipline, which is why she's free to have fun. But I found that American actors are intensely disciplined and extremely hard-working.'

Reese did her best to fit in with the largely British cast but revealed that the leading men frequently turned their mischievous humour on their American co-star. 'You have to hold your own around Rupert and Colin because they'll give you a hard time,' she told the *Mirror*. 'They'll run you into the ground if you let them, so I was constantly having to stick up for myself around. I was the youngest, so naturally they picked on me. They would tease me about my accent and going to Hollywood premieres. They would say they had read terrible things about me that morning in the newspapers. They had me going all day once. I was terribly upset and trying to track down the paper.'

The rivalry works on screen in the stream of barbed banter as well as a playful tussle over a crumpet at afternoon tea. On one occasion the clashing actors even got carried away while picking bluebells in the woods. 'We picked bluebells together and started to argue, and then it got physical,' said Colin to the *Hollywood Reporter*. 'I scrunched his bunch of bluebells, and then he pushed me over.'

'They are like The Odd Couple, completely different

guys but very comfortable with each other, and that comes across in the film,' said producer Barnaby Thompson in the *Sunday Express*.

Asked in interviews about their previous rift, Colin initially insisted that 'This time everything was fine'.

'Even though there was an eighteen-year gap, there was a bizarre familiarity immediately,' he told the *Express* in 2002. 'I do remember a strange look of recognition between us when we met again. We were a bit like an old married couple.'

And although he admitted they hadn't got together since, he said there were plans to do so and that the relationship now had 'social potential'. In February 2003, during a press conference in his adopted city of Rome, he appeared to be saying the feud was still alive and well. However, as he conducted the interview, impressively, in Italian, a mix-up over tenses may have appeared in the translation.

'Personally I've never been able to stand Rupert very much,' he reportedly told the gathered European journalists. 'But on set we managed to get on really very well. Rupert and I hate each other because we are basically very different. I find him a frightfully sophisticated person. He's improved a little with age; he's certainly not become more serious but more tolerant.'

In another interview he expressed irritation that Rupert had revealed their earlier rows. 'We didn't take to each other, but this is a story that I would have never revealed to the public if he hadn't done so during the promotion of the film in the States.'

The two actors would bury the hatchet for good six years later, when Rupert asked Colin to star in his pet project, a remake of *St Trinian's*.

people doing that for them. I had to get in there and say, "Wait, Renée, don't! You're making me look bad!"'

As well as enjoying time in amiable company, Colin was happy with the way the film was going. 'I think this film is very funny, funnier than the last,' he said to *Glamour*. 'If the first one had bombed then we'd never have made this second film, but it was a sort of unwritten rule that if the first was successful we'd all agree to do another one. I also like getting the chance to take a swing at that obnoxious Hugh Grant again!'

The banter between the two actors reached a new high when the DVD of *Love Actually* was released in 2004. His light-hearted commentary constantly aimed digs at Colin's acting, his looks and his ageing physique. 'Hugh is a brilliant raconteur, a very funny guy,' Colin conceded. 'He has a go at me from the beginning to the end so much so that the legal department at Universal sent me a copy just in case I wanted to nix anything. He basically sighs or snores whenever I appear on the scene, makes comments about how the actress is having to do all the work, or how I must be using a rinse to colour my hair, or being photographed cleverly to make my jawline look better. I like to think of it as a Bette Davis–Joan Crawford sort of thing.'

Asked which of the *Whatever Happened to Baby Jane?* actresses he would be he laughed. 'I would probably say that I'm capable of confining Hugh to a wheelchair and serving him rats. Let him take the Joan Crawford role.'

Away from the *Bridget Jones* set, their paths rarely crossed, but Colin found his name being constantly mentioned in the same breath as Hugh's. So much so that, referring to his co-star's ex-girlfriend, he told one journalist, 'I feel as if I've turned into a replacement Liz Hurley. My name's always being linked with Hugh's. Do you think there's something in it? I actually hardly know the poor man, although I'm sure we'd make a lovely couple.'

In March 2004 Colin achieved a comedy badge of honour when he was asked to be the guest host on *Saturday Night Live*. He introduced himself as 'the stuffy alternative' to Hugh Grant.

The comedy on and off screen merely made both men more beloved by the British public. *Bridget Jones: The Edge of Reason* was released in November 2004 to mixed reviews, but the actors won the heartiest praise. Christopher Tookey, in the *Daily Mail*, said, 'In Firth, Grant and Paul Bettany (who stood head and shoulders above the mediocrity of the film *Wimbledon*), Britain has the world's three best rom-com actors.'

Bridget had undoubtedly boosted Colin's career but he was still keen to draw a line under the Darcy phenomenon and move on.

He stopped short of ruling himself out of another sequel, but he told the *Calgary Sun*, 'I'm quite content to never do another Bridget Jones movie again, I've enjoyed myself, but I want Darcy to get out of my life.'

CHAPTER 17

Man on a Mission

COLIN MAY HAVE thought his brood was noisy when they were all together but in April 2005 he walked on to a set with a lot more potential for chaos. As a widowed father of seven unruly youngsters in *Nanny McPhee*, he had accepted his first role in a fully fledged kids' movie and his co-stars included children from the ages of fifteen years to six months. Written and directed by *Love Actually* co-star Emma Thompson, and adapted from a children's book by Christianna Brand, it is the story of a magical nanny who appears at the door when the harried father is at the end of his tether and the kids are out of control.

Thomas Sangster, who had leapt to fame playing Liam Neeson's stepson in *Love Actually*, was the oldest lad. Ironically, Kelly Macdonald, who had played Colin's daughter in *My Life So Far*, now became his love interest as the family maid. Unlike many dads in the industry, Colin was initially reluctant to throw himself into a simple family movie, being habitually drawn towards complex characters.

'I'd never done a film for children of this age and I wasn't sure about it,' he told *Courier-Mail*. 'I usually play the fairly complicated characters and I wasn't sure if I was cut out for the innocence of it. Once I got over myself a bit, and it took a couple of days, I had a great time doing it.' When he arrived on set, however, his reservations disappeared. 'I thought, "This is an opportunity to have a very enjoyable time."' As a joke, he even dressed up in Nanny McPhee's Victorian nanny costume – complete with bulbous nose, crooked teeth and hairy warts – to surprise his fellow cast members.

In her wonderful diaries from the shoot, Emma Thompson recalled that her leading man needed a little coaxing to leave his darker side behind. 'Colin, who has come to us from a series of more serious pieces, has to be dragged from the dramatic into comic exaggeration like someone being pulled from a pit. He is teased mercilessly. He and Kelly are so approachable and don't seem to mind interference (mine).'

She also revealed that the script called for Colin to 'skitter', meaning to run to and fro in a blind panic, and Colin told her, 'I don't like skittering'.

On 27 April 2005, she wrote, 'I am in heaven. I am in an orchard next to Mrs Quickly's house. The children are playing with some geese. Colin jumped over a bush to grab Evangeline, and in his green frock coat he looks like a gigantic frog. Then he smoulders most effectively at her, which gave me a fright after all the comic invention. I suddenly remembered he's a sex symbol'.

Once he was busy filming in the beautiful countryside of Buckinghamshire and Dorset, Colin entered into the spirit of the film and relished the idea of making children laugh with his slapstick antics. 'Really, the film is just trying to delight all kids,' he explained. 'There is something quite uplifting about that. We are actually just trying to please children. It's that simple.'

Although targeting tots for the first time in his career, he decided not to show it to his own children, who would be five and three when it was released in October 2005.

'I don't push myself at them,' he said. 'The little ones are very little. It's weird to see a parent on the screen and I don't think I'm going to hasten towards that moment. They've seen me in magazines and on buses, but they probably think everyone's dads are on buses.'

He did take his children on set, however, just before filming a massive food fight when everyone ended up covered in brightly coloured icing. 'What looks a rollicking good time is a painstaking and drawn-out process,' he explained. 'Those things weren't edible. My children came to the set and saw all these pink and purple buns – I had to tell them not only would you break your teeth if you tried to eat one, you'd be hospitalized if you succeeded.'

While working on the movie, Colin met Angela Lansbury, who proved useful when he was researching his next role. In *Where the Truth Lies* he was to play a fading entertainer with a very dark side. His screen partner was Kevin Bacon and, although the story was fictional, the characters in the original Rupert Holmes novel were loosely based on the relationship between Dean Martin and Jerry Lewis. Angela had known the Rat Pack in the fifties, at the height of their fame, 'and she was fantastic with her advice', said Colin.

Although the part was originally for an Italian-American, like Martin, director Atom Egoyan asked Colin to play it in the style more akin to British stars David Niven and Rex

Harrison. The film is set in the seventies, fifteen years after a young woman was found dead in the double act's hotel suite. Neither was charged with the crime and they haven't spoken about it since but an investigative reporter attempts to get to the bottom of the fateful night for a book. Colin's character is a beloved entertainer and comic whose onstage persona hides a violent streak and a penchant for seedy sex.

One notorious scene called for Colin and Kevin to indulge in a threesome with the hotel maid, played by Rachel Blanchard, who is later found dead.

'Actually, I was saved by Kevin's butt,' joked the British star to the *Sydney Morning Herald*. 'I hadn't been filming the week that some solid shagging took place between Kevin and various women, so by the time I showed up there was no interest at all. The crew were so sick of the sight of his butt and mine offered nothing new. People make a lot of the sexual thing but that's really only one more weird thing we get to do.'

In fact, Colin found the spontaneous violence harder to cope with than the nudity, but he welcomed the contradiction his character represented. 'It was a chance for me to play with the perception of me that I carry around, which is the buttoned-up Englishman, well-educated, formally charming sort of chap,' he said. 'I'm a rather ropey shabby individual. What you see on stage is what you might expect to see, the educated Englishman, so when I walk off stage and beat someone to a pulp or behave with sexual excess it is more of a shock.

'It's more difficult to act violence than it is to act sex. It leaves you rather shaken. It's not an easy place to go.'

Although it was never destined to be a huge box office hit, sitting more comfortably with the art-house set, the film opened to rave reviews in October 2005 with *Empire* magazine praising 'flawless performances from Bacon and Firth'. The *Hollywood Reporter* declared, 'Firth may prove a revelation to those who have only seen him in period pictures and English comedies' and Cosmo Landesman of *The Sunday Times* called it 'a joy to watch'.

• • •

Colin's love of all things Italian was reciprocated in January 2005 when the country's president, Carlo Ciampi, bestowed a rare compliment. This most English of actors was to receive the Commander of the Order of the Star of Italian Solidarity, an honour set up to reward those who helped in the reconstruction of the country after the Second World War, and now bestowed on foreigners who promote the country abroad.

As a result, he and Livia were invited to a reception at Buckingham Palace to honour the President and his wife, hosted by the Queen and the Duke of Edinburgh, and attended by the Prince of Wales, the Duke of York and the Princess Royal, in March 2005, before he had officially received his title. Colin looked dashing in a black tailcoat but it was the ever elegant Livia who stole the show in a beautiful white dress overlaid with black lace. The Queen toasted the presidential couple with Bollinger champagne and fine Italian wine. But while she praised all things Italian in her speech, including the food, she laid on a very British spread of chicken and tomato soup, poached fillet of sea bass, saddle of lamb, new potatoes, carrots, broad beans, green and yellow baby squash, and salad, followed by vanilla and chocolate terrine, and dessert fruits.

As the Press Association's royal correspondent Peter Archer wryly observed, 'she may actually have a liking for spaghetti bolognese, but it is potentially too messy to eat in public and the Queen likes to treat her guests to traditional British fare'.

Colin was invested on 26 May, during a gala evening at the Italian Embassy in London. 'We were delighted to honour Colin Firth in this way,' said a statement from Italian ambassador Giancarlo Aragona. 'He has made a significant contribution to the promotion of Italy's image in the UK and has collaborated extensively with the Italian Cultural Institute in London in staging numerous literary events.'

The newly invested actor couldn't have been more thrilled. It was a clear indication that the country he had grown to love so much had truly accepted him into their fold.

'Italy has become a big part of my life now,' he said. 'I love it. It's a huge blessing. I sort of married a whole family and a whole country. And learning Italian is a huge bonus that I didn't expect. I thought I was doomed to be unilingual for the rest of my life, like most Englishmen.'

As well as considering himself fortunate to have learned a language, he is a huge lover of Italian food and admires their attitude towards dining.

'I was very lucky to marry into the right cuisine,' he told *The Observer*. 'I've got nothing against Polish cuisine but it would have been a less joyous union if I'd married a Polish girl. Italians aren't snobbish about food. But they have rules and they don't understand when people break them – like ordering a cappuccino after dinner. I think the Italian attitude to food is genetic. Livia knows how to fillet a fish on the plate in a second. If we are having fish, everybody's plate looks like a train wreck except hers.'

Like the Queen, however, he is reluctant to try and beat the Italians at their own game, and has revealed that being married to Livia has meant staying out of the kitchen rather than learning the art of cuisine.

'I cook less now, because I am so intimidated by being surrounded by such cooking genius,' he admitted to the *Irish Times*. 'I am very cautious about putting in my own contribution.'

Whether Livia would want him banging about in the kitchen is debatable too. While he considers himself reasonably domesticated and tidy in most respects, his attempts at whipping up a family meal tend to mean a lot of clearing up.

'I'm married to an Italian who is a phenomenal cook, and far more fastidiously tidy than I am,' he told *The Independent on Sunday*. 'I tend to make an outrageous mess in the kitchen. I like to think the results are OK but the process is pretty grisly.'

Colin's principles, rather than his culinary skills, saw him taking on the catering trade in 2005. Shortly after being pictured covered in coffee for Oxfam's Make Trade Fair campaign, the socially conscious actor became a director of a chain of coffee shops which aimed to do just that. Progreso, part owned by Oxfam, was to launch across London high streets and challenge the likes of Starbucks while giving coffee farmers in developing countries a share of the profits. And Colin was not just a famous figurehead. He took his responsibilities seriously, travelling to Ethiopia to meet the producers directly affected by the West's tendency to pay below the odds for their beans.

It was, he told *The Independent*, 'a very sobering education. 'I'd read all the reports, done my homework, digested the facts,' he continued. 'But actually meeting people whose dream is simply to earn enough to buy a tin roof or send their kids to school, makes it real. You're faced with emotional implications, the sheer and simple unfairness of it all.'

Determined not to be just 'another celebrity in Africa', he also put his money where his mouth is, investing a lump sum into the set-up costs and even buying shares in the company for the farmers themselves. He also lobbied the World Trade Organization to put pressure on the high-profit coffee firms, such as Kraft and Nestlé, and handed in a petition with seven million signatures. He travelled to Glasgow to visit the roasting plant, and even did a day's training so he could serve behind the counter in the Portobello Road cafe. 'Having Mr Darcy serve the coffee is a practical way of using my profile without giving everyone earache,' he remarked. 'People seemed to think there was nothing more normal than having me serve their cappuccinos and espressos.'

A second trip to Ethiopia left him humbled by the attitude of the poverty-stricken farmers. 'I was greeted with enormous grace and then their boss who was high in the union leadership said something that stayed with me for the rest of the trip. "Three times we've been visited by well-meaning people," he said, "and nothing has changed." It was very chastening and I came to see how close my visit was to being bogus and ineffectual. I knew I had to have something to say for myself or I'd just be another disaster tourist.'

Colin was honest with the man and told him he couldn't guarantee change but would do his utmost to get the farmers' voices heard. Then he asked what message his host, the leader of the Coche Co-op, would like to send. What he and his fellow growers asked for was not charity, just a fair price for their product. 'Whenever we told Ethiopians that the price of a cup of coffee on the high street is as much as £2.75, there was this incredulous laughter and then they shook their heads with worldly resignation. It takes twenty-four beans to make a cup of coffee and yet in a bad year the producer is selling a kilo of beans for just 5p. So who is making the profit? Not the farmer.'

Despite their poverty Colin was uplifted by the optimism of the Ethiopians he met: 'It's so troubled as a country but the people we met were friendly and eloquent, which made me feel even more useless. No one projected misery or despondency, far less than on Oxford Street, actually. I met the owner of a little wooden hut with "Art Gallery" written in crude paint strokes. He showed us his plans to build a million-pound hotel looking down over Addis. It struck me as remarkable that a man who was lucky to have enough to get him to the end of day still had this kind of dream.'

In June 2005 Colin and Richard Curtis made a surprise visit to the House of Commons to lobby the latest intake of MPs and to persuade as many as possible to attend a Make Poverty History march in Edinburgh. The rally coincided with the global concert Live 8, and was aimed at persuading the delegates at the G8 summit, which was due to meet in the Scottish capital the following week, to take action against Third World poverty.

One female MP, reported *The Independent*, was quite taken with her persuasive lobbyist. 'It was all a bit preachy, but I'd much prefer to have dishy Colin Firth on my case than Bob Geldof,' she said.

Colin did meet some opposition though. He commented, 'Most of them seemed to listen carefully, but one young Tory was quite violently opposed. We're trying to combat indifference.'

When not espousing worthy causes Colin was preparing for a period drama far from the niceties of *Pride and Prejudice*. In *The Last Legion* he was a Roman soldier charged with protecting a child emperor, played by his *Nanny McPhee* screen son, Thomas Sangster.

Coincidentally Thomas is just four months older than Colin's oldest son, Will, so playing the paternal hand wasn't too much of a stretch.

'We're in a bit of a father and son role there as well really,' Colin revealed in October 2005. 'It's ancient Rome so I'm appointed to guard this last child emperor at the moment where the whole thing collapses. Apparently this is true, that the Goths, when they finally did sack Rome, spared the life of the Emperor because he was so young. We don't know any more, but the writer just supposed, "Well, what about the guy who was sworn to protect him? Is he going to carry on protecting him even though he's not the Emperor any more?" It's about that kind of relationship.'

Shot in the autumn of 2005 in Slovakia and Tunisia, it meant months away from home. But it was not this fact that almost made him turn down the role. While Brad Pitt caused a sensation in a mini leather skirt in Troy, Colin was determined not to repeat the revealing outfit and almost backed out over the costume.

'Whether you have the build or not, you can be killed in a costume,' he fretted to the *Daily Record*. 'Russell Crowe didn't look ridiculous, but even if you have the most incredible physique there is still the danger of looking comical flaunting it in a skirt. You might become some kind of cheesy erotic fantasy. It is dangerous if you have beautiful legs and dangerous if you have legs like pipe cleaners. I can leave you to guess what applies to me.'

Luckily, it seems the Romans had invented tailoring just before the fall of the Empire. 'I'm not in a skirt,' he sighed with relief. 'Thank God, history was on our side. I was going to turn it down on the grounds of costume alone, then I got shown lots of fifth-century Romans in trousers. I thought, if that's where we're going it's fine.'

Despite an impressive cast, which also included John Hannah, Kevin McKidd and Ben Kingsley, the £40 million Roman romp failed to light a candle at the box office.

While Colin was visiting ancient Rome, a new Mr Darcy was hitting the big screen. Matthew Macfadyen took on the role of the Austen hero opposite Keira Knightley's Elizabeth Bennet for the movie version of *Pride & Prejudice*. Firth fans instantly dismissed the possibility that anyone could step into the tight breeches of their 'dear boy' but Colin was secretly hoping the usurper would steal the crown.

At the premiere of *Nanny McPhee*, Colin admitted he hadn't seen the recently released film but added, 'I hear Matthew is fantastic. I knew he would be. That role was terrific to me ten years ago but I think it's other people, not me, who have found it weird that someone else should play it. I played Hamlet once and I've seen others play that, too. I don't own the Darcy role and never wanted to. I'm very happy to let as brilliant an actor as Matthew take on the mantle.'

Sadly for Colin, the film was met with endless comparisons to his own legendary Darcy, and he usually came out on top.

'I was hoping that would bury it at a crossroads at midnight with a stake through its heart but it didn't quite do that,' he said.

With ten years of Darcymania following him around like a 'school nickname you can't shake', Colin was finally coming to terms with his sex symbol status. 'At the time of the whole *Pride and Prejudice* thing I was at odds with it really,' he reflected. 'But now I'm ageing I say, "Enjoy it and milk it, man."'

CHAPTER 18

Father and Mamma

A T THE AGE of forty-five, Colin had over thirty films and several TV roles, including the dashing Mr Darcy, under his belt. But he insists he is far from a workaholic.

'People think you never stop, but the reality is I have an average of two films a year,' he explained in 2005 to the *Daily Record*. 'I used to do a lot more films back to back before I had a family of my own. They are my reason for paring it down a bit.' He also wanted to avoid being too prolific, in case the public got tired of seeing his face on the screen. 'I think people do need a break from you. If there is a Bridget Jones film out, you are on the side of every bus. I get sick of being stuck in traffic in London and getting overtaken by a bus with my face on the side.'

Having worked solidly since leaving drama school at the age of twenty-two, he was aware of how lucky he has been and has often noted that the ease of his path to fame, without the years touring in rep that other actors often endure at the beginning of their careers, occasionally gave him pangs of guilt. 'There is an unease,' he told Sue Lawley on *Desert Island Discs*. 'I was brought up with a lot of Protestant values and you're supposed to pay your dues somewhere. Perhaps your soul needs a bit of hardship to develop so I do wonder when the catch is to come.'

It wasn't coming any time soon. In 2006 Colin was very much in demand and about to embark on a bumper year with two TV movies and several high-profile films in the pipeline. He began the year in London, filming the television version of Harold Pinter's *Celebration* and a gritty drama about homelessness, *Born Equal.* In the latter, he plays a wealthy hedge fund manager whose conscience is pricked by an aggressive encounter with a homeless man. To assuage his guilt, he begins to help out at a local shelter where he meets a group of people whose lives are a million miles away from his own, including a teenage runaway (Nichola Burley), a Nigerian asylum seeker (David Oyelowo) and a violent ex-con (Robert Carlyle). Directed by Dominic Savage, to mark the twentieth anniversary of the revolutionary drama *Cathy Come Home*, the film was largely improvised, which was a new experience for Colin.

'Dominic doesn't even rehearse,' he told *The Independent*. 'He just switches on the camera and says: "Go for it." It's like jumping into a freezing pool – you just hope you pop up again alive.' He found it hard to identify with his character, who treats his pregnant wife with contempt and rarely thinks of the hurt he causes others, and he confessed he would never be able to do Mark's job in real life. 'I wouldn't understand what a hedge fund manager does even if you sat me down and explained it to me for an entire lifetime,' he said. 'Anything financial gets actors into a complete terror. I start to suffocate when I see numbers on a screen. It takes me right back to that utter inability to get anywhere with maths O level.'

While he has thrown his weight behind campaigns for the rights of asylum seekers and Third World coffee growers, he admitted he had often overlooked the plight of his own countrymen. 'Getting into detail about how some people do live, right on my doorstep – the traps that people find themselves in – was sobering and it did give me a jolt,' he said to the *Sunday Express*. 'My wife has had a subscription to the homeless charity Shelter for a long time. I have tended to put my energies in a different direction, though this has woken me up on homelessness. I can't say that I came to a new judgement, but I'm a little more aware. I will remember that the next time I walk past a homeless person. I hope that is the effect of the film; that it will lodge itself as a reference point and have some way of working its way in as the years go by.'

Another thought-provoking drama kept Colin at home in the late summer. *When Did You Last See Your Father?* is a tender family story based on the memoirs of Blake Morrison, who wrote the book when grieving over the loss of his own dad. On learning his father has been diagnosed with terminal cancer, Blake returns to the small village where he grew up to help his mother and sister care for the old man. During his stay he looks back over the troubled relationship of the two men, and their failure to connect on an emotional level.

Blake's father Arthur is a domineering, often irritating figure in his son's life and Colin said he couldn't be further from his own 'quiet, unassuming' dad. Now very close to his parents, the actor was happy to take the blame for any friction in the relationship in his younger days. 'I was a surly, pretentious adolescent, like Blake's portrait of himself,' he said. 'My father and I were not close in a cosy sense but I am as connected with my father as Blake was with his. The difference is my animosity with my dad was left behind in my teens. But, even now, three seconds in my parents' company and a tone of voice or trigger will bring me back to being fifteen.'

Like millions of viewers after him, Colin was moved to consider his own parents' mortality by the movie. 'All the stuff that the movie deals with, it's not stuff that occurred to me for the first time,' he told the *Big Issue*, 'but it does make you reflect. My parents are actually young and healthy, so it's not like time is imminently running out but the fact is, this is the time we've got and don't wait for the last minute.' In his own family, he revealed, there had been no early deaths but at the age of thirty-five he was shaken by the first loss of a grandparent: his grandfather. 'It was a shock, some part of me finding out we weren't immortal in my family.'

The film, and his role as both father and son, led to a great deal of self-analysis. 'I asked more questions about myself through this film than anything else I have ever done,' he told the *Daily Express*. 'I am both a son – my father is now seventy-three – and a father. How good have I been at both? Could I be better? It is not too late, so how can I change?'

Dad David loved the film so much he went to see it a second time. 'He's very into the questions that it asks, partly because he's just lost his father and probably feels more like a son when he watches,' said Colin. 'He's not a demonstrative, loquacious person, he keeps very much to himself in a way but was very moved by the film. I haven't really sat down with him – this is one of the things you don't do, sit down and have that conversation. Blake sits at Arthur's bedside and they're going through bills!'

The scenes when Blake cringes as his father charms a bar full of drinkers struck a chord with Colin, making him think of his relationship with sixteen-year-old Will. 'I think I'm probably the kind of father more like Arthur than Blake,' he pondered. 'I'm no shrinking violet myself and I dare say that his toes curl when I'm thinking I'm being charming.'

While his own scenes are powerful and moving, Colin felt a flash of recognition for those which starred Matthew Beard as the young Blake. The simple pleasures of a childhood in the sixties came flooding back. 'Washing the car on a Sunday, having iodine put on your cuts, putting a tent up come hell or high water – the whole thing resonated,' he recalled. 'Camping trips in the rain were not unusual when I was growing up. To me, though, there was never any recreation about freezing rain in a field . . .'

Released in October, *When Did You Last See Your Father?* won rave reviews, with Peter Bradshaw of *The Guardian* moved by this 'deeply felt' drama and Christopher Tookey of the *Daily Mail* called it a 'well-crafted, beautifully acted little film'. It also landed six nominations at the British Independent Film Awards and, perhaps more importantly, managed to reduce grown men to tears in cinemas all over the country and had them straight on the phone to their dads.

Colin had barely finished filming before he was on a plane to the New York for back-to-back rom-coms. *Then She Found Me* was a pet project for Helen Hunt, who had spent eight years adapting Elinor Lipman's book and bringing it to the big screen. The central character, played by Helen, is a schoolteacher suffering a midlife crisis after her husband leaves and her biological mother, a chat show host who had her adopted as a baby, tracks her down. The actress-turned

-director almost rejected Colin for the role of the father of a student whom the teacher falls for because she thought he was too good-looking.

'I think I was afraid, and he was afraid, that he's so appealing that the minute he comes on screen you'd stop worrying about April,' she said. 'If he showed up and was just so perfect and dreamy that all of her problems were over, the movie would have been over ten minutes in. I actually wrote the part for someone much less tall, handsome and appealing.'

After wrapping, Colin stayed in the Big Apple for *The Accidental Husband*, playing the publisher fiancé of radio agony aunt Uma Thurman.

Both hitting the screens in 2007, the movies were received with very different reviews. *Then She Found Me* was largely praised and Colin's performance as the single dad riding to the rescue of the emotionally battered April won critics over on both sides of the Atlantic. 'Frank (Colin Firth) is any woman's dream, a manly but sensitive and witty soul whose first wife must have been insane to leave him,' gushed Philip Marchand in the *Toronto Star*. *The Observer*'s Rex Reed declared, 'The Hunt–Firth team has a glowing chemistry.' Fluffy rom-com *The Accidental Husband*, however, saw *Sunday Express* critic Henry Fitzherbert slamming Colin for playing 'another stiff Brit in a picture that will do him no favours' and *The Telegraph*'s Tim Robey commenting that it 'lacks the faintest spark of originality'.

In between his many filming commitments, Colin found time to take up the cudgel on behalf of his mother's pet cause, fighting for the right of asylum seekers. In February 2007 he joined forces with Shirley's charity, the Southampton and Winchester Visitors' Group, and five prominent bishops to campaign against the deportation of a Congolese nurse who called himself Pierre. The young man had fled to Britain after being tortured and jailed for refusing to administer lethal morphine doses to political opponents of the military leaders. After hearing about the case from Shirley, Colin personally contacted the newspapers to publicize the man's plight.

'Nobody likes an actor with a cause, least of all me,' Colin told *The Independent*. 'But there is good reason to believe this guy is at risk. He is certain that if he returns he will be murdered.'

The army nurse had escaped the Democratic Republic of Congo after his brother bribed guards at the jail, and had been living in the UK, sleeping on friends' floors, for five years after his application for asylum was turned down. As the Labour government prepared to fly him home, along with another forty other failed asylum seekers, Colin could not contain his anger. 'It just makes me so furious,' he said. 'There's going to be nineteen kids on this flight, a chartered plane because they don't want kids kicking and screaming on a commercial flight when they bundle them out through the back door.

'This man has been exemplary. To me it's just basic civilization to help people. I find this incredibly painful to see how we dismiss the most desperate people in our society. It's easily done. It plays to the tabloids, to the middle-England xenophobes. It just makes me furious. And all from a government we once had such high hopes for.'

In a letter to *The Guardian* Colin wrote, 'There is considerable evidence of the dangers of returning to the DRC. It is imperative that this particular deportation is stopped; but this case represents a wider problem of wholesale deportations of asylum seekers. This man is a nurse who has been in the UK for five years and behaved perfectly while here. Now, instead of making badly needed use of his nursing skills, our government is prepared to connive at his murder.'

In a plot twist worthy of a Hollywood movie, Pierre and three others received a last-minute reprieve, even as the plane stood on the tarmac at Stansted airport. A legal appeal was successful and he was allowed to remain in the UK. 'I am overjoyed because we have worked very hard for him,' said Shirley, on hearing the news. 'He had a very good case and would have been in danger if he had been sent back. There is a culture of disbelief at the Home Office in assessing applications from refugees. It doesn't always try to get at what the truth is.'

After railing against the government over asylum seekers, Colin turned to pure anarchy – on the set of *St Trinian's*. Oddly enough, it was his old adversary Rupert Everett who approached him to star as a starchy school inspector, having come up with the idea of remodelling the classic comedy series for a modern audience. Rupert was playing the dual role of headmistress Miss Fritton and her brother Carnaby, as played by Alastair Sim in the original movies. Colin was Geoffrey Thwaites, an old flame who is now determined to instil discipline into the unruly schoolgirls or shut the place down.

Working together at Ealing Studios, the pair finally made their peace and became good friends. Colin, whom Rupert nicknamed Frothy, acknowledged their past difficulties but said they was now firmly in the past. 'It wasn't really a feud or a war of words. It was a war of stony silences,' he said in an interview with the author. 'It didn't really go beyond the end of that film in 1983. We didn't really see each other for eighteen years.'

Buoyed by their new camaraderie, Rupert wrote a

foreword for the paperback version of his autobiography, *Red Carpets and Banana Skins*, putting Colin's side of the fallout on *Another Country*. 'Colin Firth says he did not bring a guitar to the set of *Another Country* and that, even if he did, he never learnt to play "Lemon Tree". Last week, on the set of *St Trinian's*, which we are filming as this tome goes to print, he went even further and categorically swore that he had never worn sandals (without socks, maybe),' he wrote. But he couldn't resist a side swipe, concluding, 'Reinvention is the celebrity spring clean.'

One scene called for the two actors to end up in bed together, and the new relationship was sealed with a kiss.

'We are getting on terribly well, especially now that we have finally been united as lovers,' Rupert told the *Sunday Telegraph*. 'Although I think Colin took it a little bit too seriously – he wanted to do take after take of the snog scene. I suppose he's always been rather in love with me.'

In turn, Colin revealed that the scene had 'rather surprised me. Rupert turned into a giggling schoolboy. He was adamant that we shouldn't kiss; I was adamant that we should. But the chemistry was definitely there in the end.'

Surrounded by beautiful young girls, including Gemma Arterton, Talulah Riley and Lily Cole, the older pair were the ones indulging in the juvenile pranks on set. On one occasion, when Colin was due to grope Miss Fritton's chest, Rupert stuck inflated balloons up his costume in the hope they would burst and put Colin off. When the prank went wrong he let his co-star in on the joke. 'Next time, he put pins in his fingers so he burst them when he grabbed me,' recalled Rupert. 'It certainly startled the crew.'

Colin remembered watching the original films as a child and being frightened of the miniskirted temptresses of the girls' school. 'I can't remember how old I was but I was probably under ten when I saw these films and I was very attracted to then, and very frightened of them, which is quite an explosive combination,' he said in an interview with the author. And he admitted the outrageous outfits worn by the young actresses in the movie were far from politically correct. 'We dress our children up in this bizarre way, which has a quasi-adult feeling about it so it endows them with a precocious kind of adulthood,' he said. 'Then we complain when people fetishize them. We're not in a safe PC area, definitely, but it's something that has been a central part of English culture for decades. So yes, there is a slightly pervy element to the whole thing.'

Colin went from the anarchic romp of *St Trinian's* to some fun in the sun in *Mamma Mia!* Filming in Greece coincided with the low-budget *Genova*, which, being shot entirely in Italy, persuaded Colin to break his own rule on avoiding work during the boys' summer holidays. The two films could not have been more different in tone. The first is a joyous star-studded love story set on a Greek island, punctuated with Abba songs, and the second the tragic tale of a grieving dad who moves his family to an Italian city in an attempt to get over the death of his wife.

In *Mamma Mia!* Colin played one of three potential fathers to Meryl Streep's daughter, played by Amanda Seyfried. In the run-up to her wedding, she invites mum Donna's past lovers to their Aegean hideaway in an attempt to discover which one is her real dad, so that he can give her away on the day. Pierce Brosnan and Stellan Skarsgård were cast as the other two possible parents while Julie Walters and Christine Baranski jumped on board as Donna's best pals.

For the part of 'Headbanger Harry' Colin would have

to sing, dance and even play his beloved guitar, and he joked that his singing voice is 'somewhere between a drunken apology and a plumbing problem'.

He admitted he hadn't been required to sing seriously since he led the 'ropey schoolboy band' of his youth but he had no fear of being judged for his dulcet tones.

'If they'd wanted Broadway-level dancers and singers they would've cast people like John Travolta,' he argued. 'They didn't: it's myself, Pierce Brosnan and Stellan Skarsgård.'

The most mortifying thing, he quipped, was the Spandex suit he had to wear for the final payoff on the film. 'There are bulges where there should not be bulges and no bulges where you wish there were.' While filming the musical on the picturesque Greek island of Skopelos, co-star Pierce hinted at a little competition between himself and Colin.

'I do a lot of singing and dancing and, yes, I'm good at it, even at my age,' said the Bond star. 'The knees are still good, the back is still good and the ego is fine. Colin is a lot more nimble than I am. It's going to be a tough battle.'

As a glam rock fan in the seventies, Colin had not been a huge fan of Abba and claimed, 'Few straight males of my generation would have put their hands up and claimed to have been an Abba fan. If I'd had a crystal ball in 1976 and seen this is the sort of thing I'd end up doing, I would have ended it all at that moment.'

In an appearance on US TV, he revealed that the movie was so camp 'it will make *Sex and the City* look like *Iron Man*. It's going to be huge.' His prediction was spot on.

The movie was to become his biggest box office success to date, even outstripping *Bridget Jones*, with a massive £365 million ($600 million) worldwide.

Although it meant fitting in scenes around his *Mamma*

Mia! work, *Genova* ticked all the right boxes. As well as shooting in Italy, Colin got to play an academic, a role that would come easily to someone who grew up around academia, and he was playing a father. It was also a small independent film using a small crew and directed by Michael Winterbottom, whom he was keen to work with.

'It's a different area emotionally from anything else Michael's done,' he said. 'It's a different tone, and he seems to be endlessly curious. He's got no snobbery. He would do exactly what fascinated him. He's one of the few people I can honestly say that I was dying to work with, and that's not just the usual spiel. I think everybody would be interested in working with Michael.'

Flitting between the big-budget Hollywood set on the beaches of Greece and the low-budget art-house film in the beautiful city of Genoa provided an interesting couple of months for the busy actor, and he felt the *Genova* set brought him firmly back down to earth. 'It couldn't be more contrasting,' he said. 'There were moments when I got a chill, partly because you are filming in such real circumstances. You're in real rooms, you have a whole run of scenes and you're staring at what you're supposed to be staring at. So if it's 3 a.m., dark and you're playing a scene where you hear something, it's sort of real ...'

While *Mamma Mia!* was set to be the hottest hit of the year in 2008, *Genova* suffered the opposite fate, with lukewarm reviews and little box office traffic. Colin, as always, had moved on by then. He was about to return to both Coward and Wilde and, as soon as he returned to London, he and Livia had a new green business venture to keep them busy.

CHAPTER 19

A Singular Success

As Colin was beavering away on the films in Italy and Greece in August 2007, Livia and her brother Nicola were drawing up the last details of their plans to launch an environmentally friendly store of their own, with the help of Colin and entrepreneur Ivo Coulson. Eco, which opened in Chiswick High Road in September 2007, is a stylish four-storey department store specializing in green, fair-trade products and described as Britain's first 'ecological destination store'.

Colin modestly described himself as 'a handy communications device' while Livia called him 'an essential part of the project'. And she revealed the passion behind all the projects he threw himself into, and the great meeting of minds that made their marriage work.

Livia had also been busy working as executive producer on a movie highlighting the plight of a man who'd been on death row, after a flawed trial, for twenty-five years. Colin invested in the project, *In Prison My Whole Life*, which highlights flaws in the trial of Mumia Abu-Jamal, convicted of the murder of a Philadelphia policeman in 1981.

'We are a political family,' she said. 'Colin's one of those people who researches everything properly. He'll get obsessed with something like the Iraq war and then wake up in the middle of the night wanting to talk about it. We're a great match because I'm the ballbreaker and he's the brains.'

Livia's little brother Nicola, who has a PhD in alternative energy, was happy to join his sister in taking charge of the project. And he remembered his childhood as being organic and eco-friendly long before it was on the political agenda. 'Even fifteen years ago, our parents used energy-saving bulbs that took half an hour to emit light,' he recalled. 'We ate local, organic food. Nothing was thrown away. But that's just how it was in Italy.'

The store, powered by solar panels, displayed everything from environmentally friendly cleaning products to £3,000 designer chairs made from sustainable wood. In the basement, Nicola ran a consultancy service, where customers could see samples of eco-friendly flooring, tiles, pipes and radiators and get advice on building with sustainable products. 'We want this to be a good place to meet, and enjoy, as well as learn how to improve the planet,' said Nicola. 'And to do that it has to be fashionable, to have things for all generations. It can't be an eco-nutter place or it won't work.'

Colin, who admitted he was no 'eco hero', backed the family's idea to launch the shop because he felt that, as a consumer, he was complicit in the damage that Western buying habits had on the environment and the developing countries. 'The thing is, if you have been given the privileges we have, if you have this many perks, surely you can help out,' he told *The Times*. 'Rather than being a luvvie with a lofty opinion preaching to people, I prefer to do things, to get involved, put my money where my mouth is and learn along the way.'

But while he was happy to help out with the publicity, the 'unlikely shopkeeper' was not going to be caught behind the till, having learned his limitations during stints at the coffee shop. 'I worked in the cafe when it opened and the coffees I made were probably the worst we ever served,' he said. And he joked that he would appear in a Darcy-like wet shirt only if it were 'eco cotton and recyclable water. Depends how badly we need the customers. At the moment, I've got three films out and all anyone wants to talk about is the shop. So, hopefully, another drenching won't be necessary.'

The couple celebrated their tenth wedding anniversary in the summer before the opening, and Colin's admiration for his intelligent and beautiful wife was still evident. She was the one he sought out for career advice because, he said, 'she's the smartest woman on the planet'. And he revealed the secret of their happy marriage.

'We're very committed on a daily basis to how we deal with our family lives. But the real secret is time – we have to make sure that we spend enough time together. Every relationship in life you're going to have to take care of, there's a marathon factor to it.'

Colin's next two projects were the classic Noël Coward comedy *Easy Virtue*, and *Dorian Gray*, based on the Oscar Wilde novel *A Portrait of Dorian Gray*. Both were based in England and both starred up-and-coming English star Ben Barnes. For the first Ben played a young aristocratic man who brings his glamorous American bride home to the disapproval of his upper-class parents, played by Colin and